SCHIRMER PERFORMANCE EDITIONS

HAL LEONARD PIANO LIBRARY

BURGMÜLLER

18 CHARACTERISTIC STUDIES

Opus 109

Edited and Recorded by William Westney

To access companion recorded performances online, visit:
www.halleonard.com/mylibrary

Enter Code
7500-8151-1470-5175

On the cover:
Landscape with Haywagon (ca. 1858)
by Valentin Ruths
(1825–1905)
©Hamburger Kunsthalle, Hamburg, Germany/
The Bridgeman Art Library

ISBN 978-1-4234-5813-5

G. SCHIRMER, *Inc.*

DISTRIBUTED BY
HAL•LEONARD® CORPORATION
7777 W. BLUEMOUND RD. P.O. BOX 13819 MILWAUKEE, WI 53213

www.musicsalesclassical.com
www.halleonard.com

CONTENTS

The price of this publication includes access to companion recorded performances online, for download or streaming, using the unique code found on the title page. Visit **www.halleonard.com/mylibrary** and enter the access code.

HISTORICAL NOTES

Johann Friedrich Burgmüller (1806–1874)

Remembered primarily as a composer of French salon music, Johann Friedrich Burgmüller was in fact German, and he seldom receives credit for his most-often-heard work. Johann Friedrich was born in Regensburg, Germany. His father, Johann August Franz Burgmüller (1766–1824), was a composer and music director who founded the Lower Rhine Music Festival in 1818. It continues today and has served as the inspiration for countless other annual music festivals around the world. Johann Friedrich's brother Norbert, who was also a composer, showed tremendous potential before his premature death at age twenty-six in 1836.

Johann Friedrich began his musical studies as a child in his hometown. He eventually moved to Kassel to study with composer Louis Spohr (1784–1859). In 1832 he moved to France, settling in Paris. Some sources say that he relocated to Paris to serve as music teacher to the children of King Louis Philippe. It is certain that he was a fine pianist and began to make a name for himself in Paris as a composer of ballet music. His ballet *La Péri*, (not to be confused with the Dukas ballet of the same name) was first performed in Paris in February 1843. An immediate success, it was performed fifty times at the Paris Opera in a span of two-and-a-half years. It opened in St. Petersburg and Moscow in 1844, in Brussels in 1847, and in New York in 1855. Johann Friedrich also collaborated with Flotow on the score of the ballet *Lady Henrietta*. But it is the music he contributed to Adolphe Adam's legendary ballet *Giselle*, the "Valse de Giselle" and the "Peasant Pas de Deux," that is most often heard and the work for which he is often not credited. Théophile Gautier, author of the book *La Péri*, called Burgmüller's music "... elegant, delicate, full of adroit and lilting melodies which linger in one's memory..."

Johann Friedrich withdrew from public life in 1844 and focused on his teaching. He wrote piano pieces for the Parisian salons—drawing rooms, or living rooms, of the aristocratic and wealthy, where educated, cultured people gathered to hear the latest music, poetry, or literature of the day. In the middle of the nineteenth century the technology did not yet exist to play recorded music in one's home. Playing an instrument was considered an essential part of a complete education; most people of means owned instruments and were able to play them. Johann Friedrich's music is part of a tremendous volume of music that was written for these players. Just as we are interested in hearing the latest new songs, people of his day were interested in bringing home the latest pieces and playing it on their pianos. His pieces are difficult enough to be interesting, yet easy enough for a good amateur pianist to master.

—*Elaine Schmidt*

LABORUM DULCE LENIMEN G. SCHIRMER

PERFORMANCE NOTES

Burgmüller's opus 109 studies have been beloved by piano teachers and students since they first appeared almost two hundred years ago, and for good reason. They exude a charming musicality, are gratifying to play and hear, and—best of all—fulfill their central pedagogical purpose: to build technical and artistic skill.

During the process of developing piano artistry in all its different aspects, we need plenty of good challenges in order to grow. But it's best if the challenges are in digestible portions and the music at hand is appealing enough that we naturally enjoy the work and are drawn to it. When music feels good in the hands, and pleases the ear and the imagination, every step along the way becomes its own reward. Burgmüller's studies have these treasurable traits, and this is the key to their continuing popularity.

Taken as a complete set, opus 109 presents a rich compendium of the technical skills needed to develop as a classical pianist: nimble passagework, colorful voicing, tonal power, wrist rotation, staccato touch, rapid chords, and more. The level of this repertoire is primarily early advanced. Students can get their first taste of real brilliance with a well-learned Burgmüller étude, and that is a heady (and highly motivating) experience. On the artistic/expressive side, Burgmüller's studies are akin to those of Stephen Heller (to whom Burgmüller dedicated this opus) in their captivating harmonic sophistication and in the effortless way with which they ease students into more mature realms of expression. Thus, mastering the studies of opus 109 is a major step in readying oneself to play with fluency and authority the more substantial works of great composers like Beethoven, Schubert, Chopin, and Schumann.

For all these reasons, the exquisite miniatures that comprise opus 109 possess timeless value for teachers, students, and audiences alike.

NOTES ON THE PRESENT EDITION

Fingering and pedaling suggestions as well as metronome markings are those of the editor. In most cases phrasing and articulation marks have been little changed from prior editions. The descriptive titles have also been retained. Though they may have been originally created by publishers and not by the composer, they are quite apt and can stimulate the imagination of performers and listeners.

Notes on Performing the Individual Studies

BOOK I

No. 1 *Confidence*
The opening piece features an intimate, Schumannesque, long-flowing melody with some dark expressive flavors. A rich singing tone is called for, well isolated from the general texture. Even when a melodic phrase is tapered, the tonal quality should remain.

No. 2 *Les perles* (Pearls)
Familiar major scales ascending and descending, but put to spectacular and very enjoyable effect. This exciting piece requires great ease, lightness, and speed, allowing each scale to be as sweeping and free as a glissando. Most of the scales start with one "big" note, deeply played and of longer duration. This lets the pianist sink into the note, making it easier to relax the wrist and release the ensuing gossamer scale. Be generous with the pedal; this frees the finger technique. *Practice Suggestion:* to achieve ultimate speed, try one-octave scale segments free of any tempo. Play the first note extra long, so the wrist can experience a total release. Then permit the scale to fall out of your hand like an easy, relaxed, rapid blur. The feeling is effortless—almost as if we had "surprised ourselves" by playing the scale.

No. 3 ***Le retour du pâtre***
(The Shepherd's Return)
A charming, pastoral character piece featuring vivid legato/staccato contrast throughout.

No. 4 ***Les bohémiens*** **(Gypsies)**
Full of humor and theatrically dark atmosphere, this makes an effective recital piece. Take to heart the "non troppo" marking and control the tempo by counting in four as indicated, not in two. Thorough arm gestures for the staccato chords will also help prevent rushing. The technical variety and the physicality of the writing make this study a joy to play. The crisp articulations combined with high drama remind one of the operas of Verdi.

No. 5 ***La source*** **(The Spring)**
A lovely and challenging study of great pedagogical value. The melody is suffused with Romantic warmth, while the pianist must execute a sequence of wrist/arm movements with precision in order to play the piece comfortably. The various rotational and lateral motions must be identified and then played with a generous commitment. Take time to coordinate each one well with the music so there are smooth "gear shifts" with no confusion.

No. 6 ***L'enjouée*** **(The Light-hearted Lass)**
Since both hands have to jump to different positions, simultaneously at times, it is advisable to memorize the piece early. Count it in three and don't rush the tempo. Note accuracy can be a bit slippery in the all-white key of C major, so practice with a firm hand.

No. 7 ***Berceuse*** **(Lullaby)**
Sensitive lyricism combines with a specific technical challenge: the gently rolling accompaniment figure requires undulating gestures using both arms in alternation. When this movement is well choreographed, the two gestures fuse into one smooth, shared motion for the arms.

No. 8 ***Agitato***
The arms coordinate in alternating motions again, this time to more brilliant and extroverted effect. Once the notes and gestures are in place, this study can go quite fast; all it takes is trust and daring. The trick is to keep the arms feeling loose, never clutching at notes.

No. 9 ***La cloche des matines*** **(The Matin Bell)**
The sonic world here is deep and full; this is a piece that invites performance in the grand style, with expansive gesturing (notably the left hand "bells" in the treble). The A-flat Major tonality adds color and the *fortissimo* climax calls for real power, without harshness.

BOOK II

No. 10 ***La vélocité*** **(Velocity)**
Here is a passage-work study that can thrill and sparkle. Since the patterns change often, it is wise and liberating to memorize early in the learning process.

No. 11 ***La sérénade*** **(Serenade)**
Relaxed and balletic arm motions will help control the dynamics in this tuneful Mendelssohnian work. When the inner voices are kept feather-light while the outer voices sing, the charm of this piece emerges.

No. 12 ***Le réveil dans les bois***
(Awakening in the Woods)
This delightful staccato study is also a sophisticated character piece with the elegant energy of ballet music. The arms must be loose and active. Be sure not to play it too fast (count it in four, not two) in order to allow its tasty wit to shine through. To me, there is an air of enchantment here, reminiscent of the rapt atmosphere of Mendelssohn's *Midsummer Night's Dream*. This shimmering effect is enhanced when the rhythm has a jaunty bounce, thereby avoiding squareness. A simple way to accomplish this is to give a slight, sharp accent to the offbeat eighth notes, thusly:

No. 13 ***L'orage*** **(The Storm)**
This is another study that can easily transport an adventurous student to the rewarding realm of bravura playing. When the tempo is pressed a bit to the edge, this storm creates excitement and drama.

No. 14 ***Refrain du gondolier***
(The Gondolier's Refrain)
The focus here is on lushness of melody and harmony. It is important to supply the same rich sonority to all melodic notes, even brief passing tones.

No. 15 *Les sylphes* (Sylphs)
This lively, colorful piece is fun to play due to the acrobatic arm movements it uses as it ranges widely over the keyboard.

No. 16 *La séparation* (Parting)
Playing the repeated chords up to tempo can cause tension to accumulate in the right arm. A good preventive is to build in a feeling of relaxation by practicing in different groupings with an exaggeratedly loose arm. Playing the left hand melody firmly also tends to liberate and relax the right arm.

No. 17 *Marche* (March)
Exuberant, high-spirited, and entertaining, this piece calls for confident arm gestures throughout. I chose not to take the repeat of measures 8-24 on the recording.

No. 18 *La fileuse* (At the Spinning Wheel)
The final study contains the most elegant and demanding passagework of the set. It shouldn't be played too fast, as it asks for gracefulness of line in addition to brilliance. Even arpeggios are expressive elements here. After the right hand anchors each quarter note well, it can relax and free up the rapid triplets, thus making the whole piece flow with greater ease.

—*William Westney*

Confidence

J. Friedrich Burgmüller
Op. 109, No. 1

a tempo
f
dimin.
riten.
p dolce

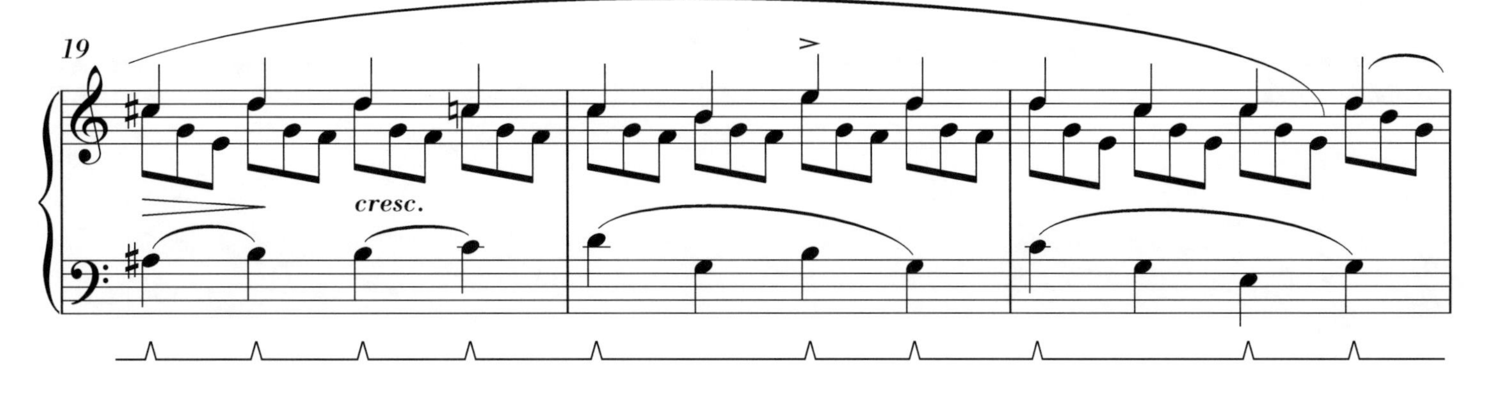
cresc.

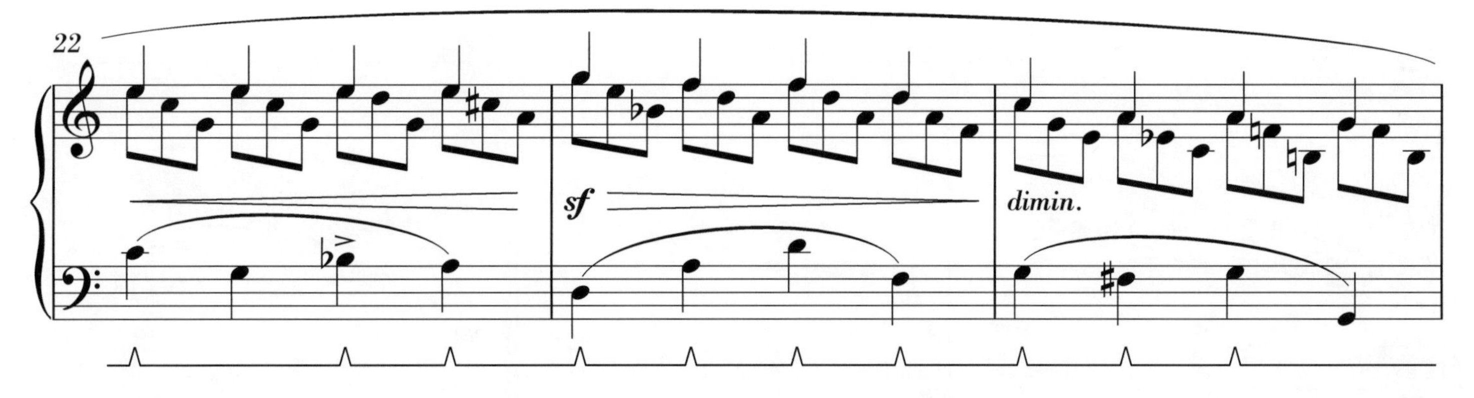
sf
dimin.

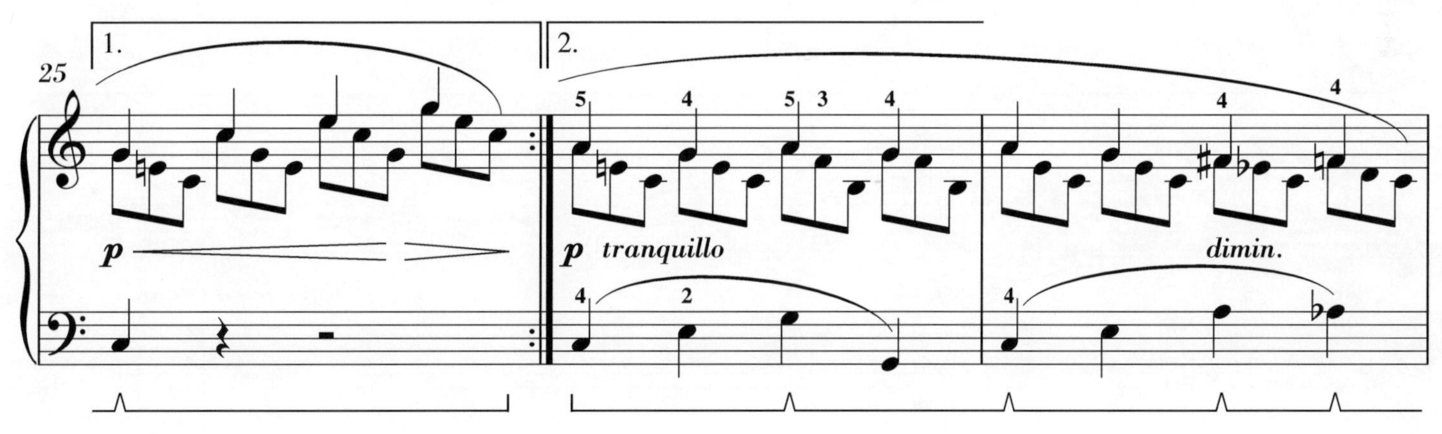
p
p tranquillo
dimin.

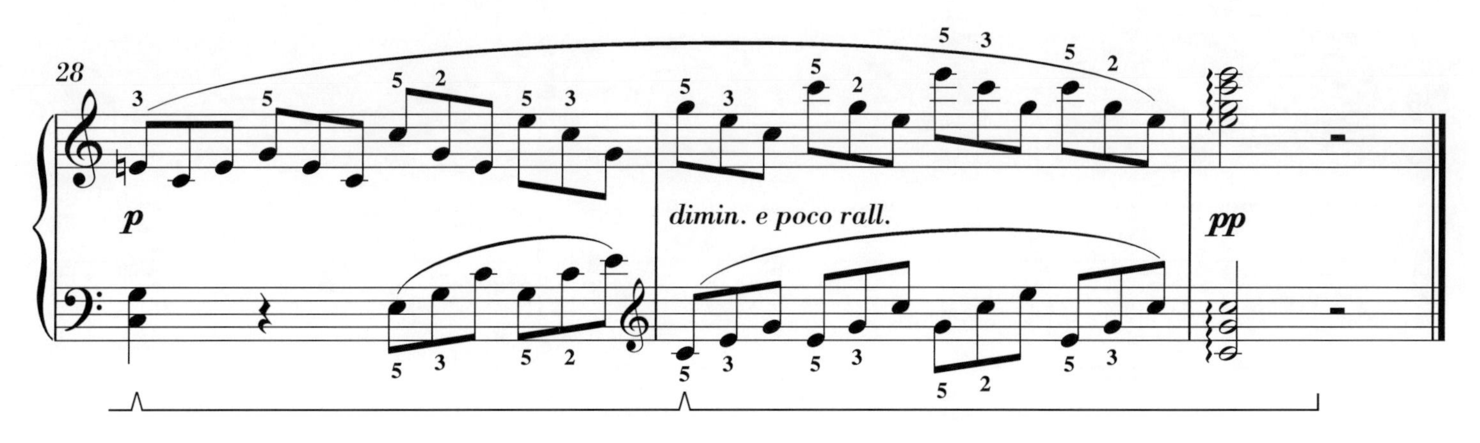
p
dimin. e poco rall.
pp

Les perles

Pearls

J. Friedrich Burgmüller
Op. 109, No. 2

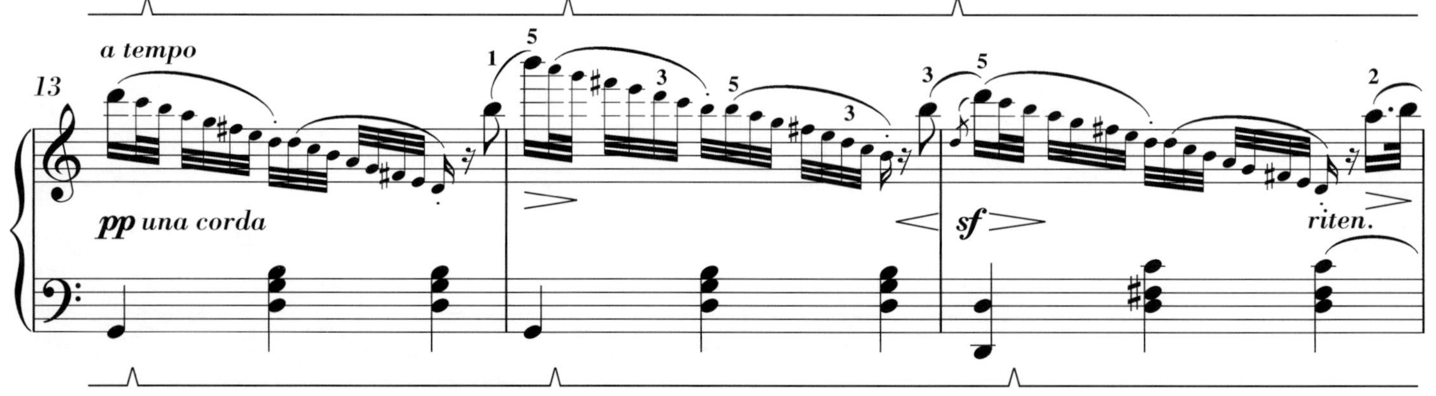

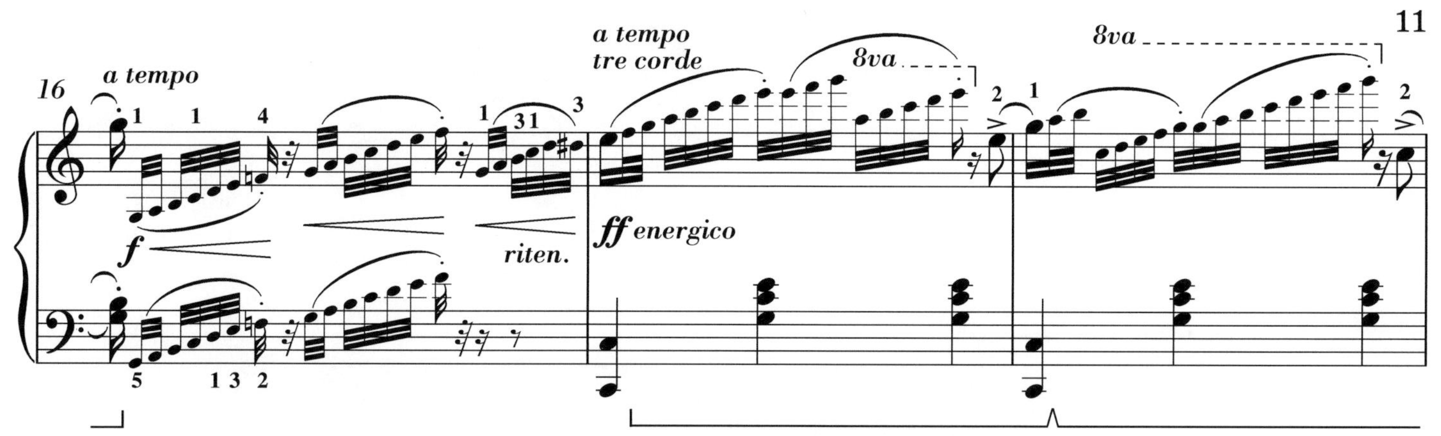
16
a tempo
f
riten.
a tempo
tre corde
8va
ff energico
8va

19
8va
8va
mf

22
dimin.
8va
8va
p

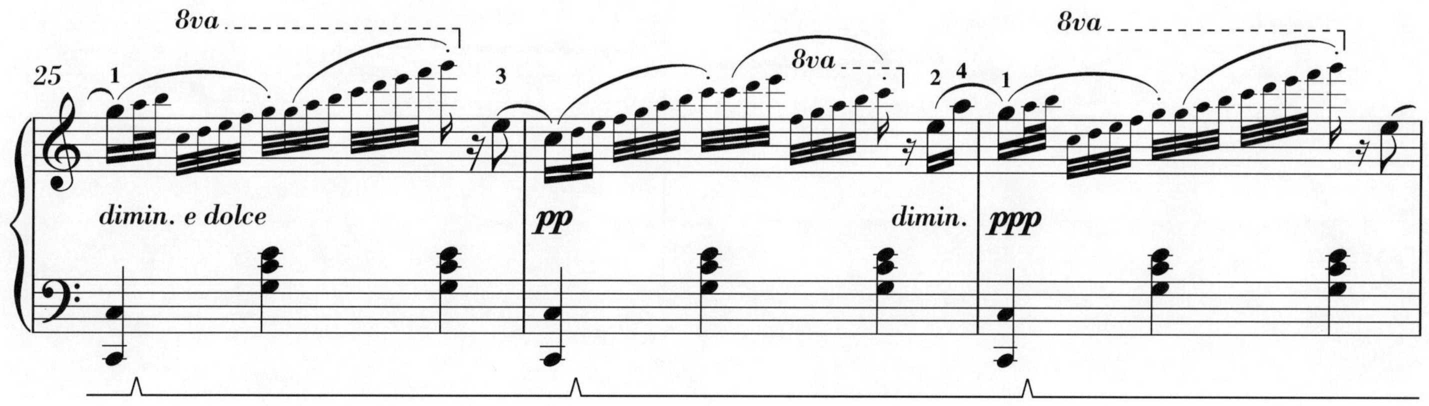
25
8va
dimin. e dolce
8va
pp
dimin.
8va
ppp

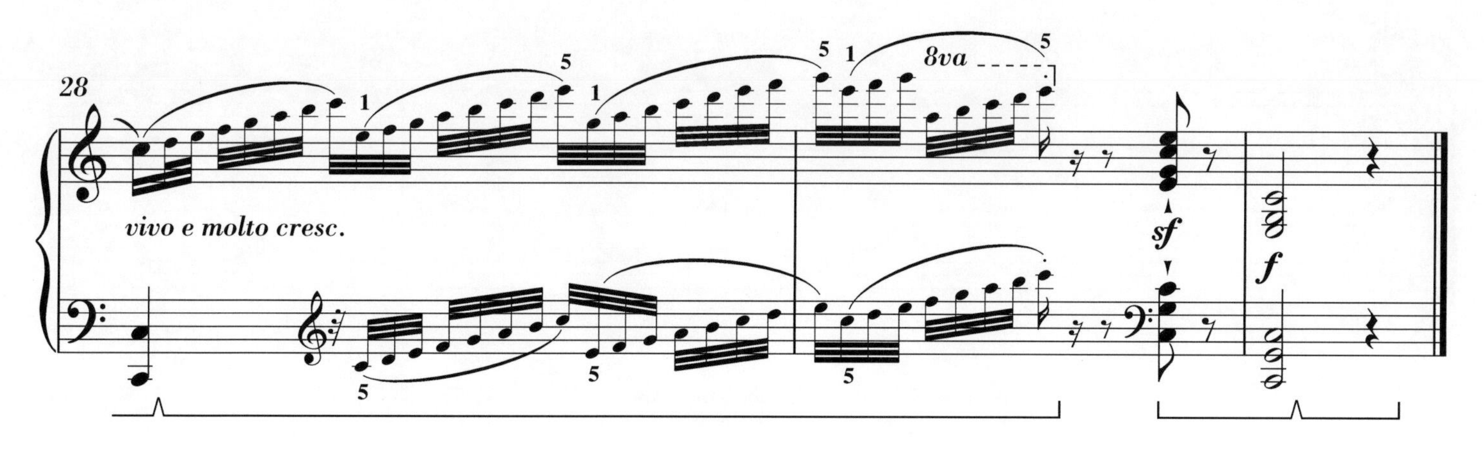
28
vivo e molto cresc.
8va
sf
f

Le retour du pâtre
The Shepherd's Return

J. Friedrich Burgmüller
Op. 109, No. 3

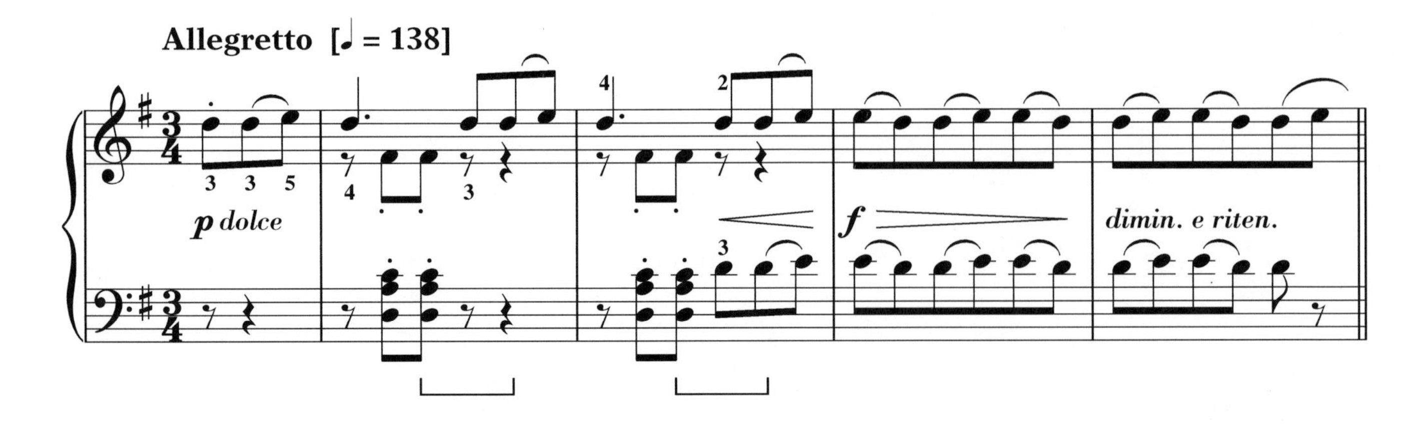

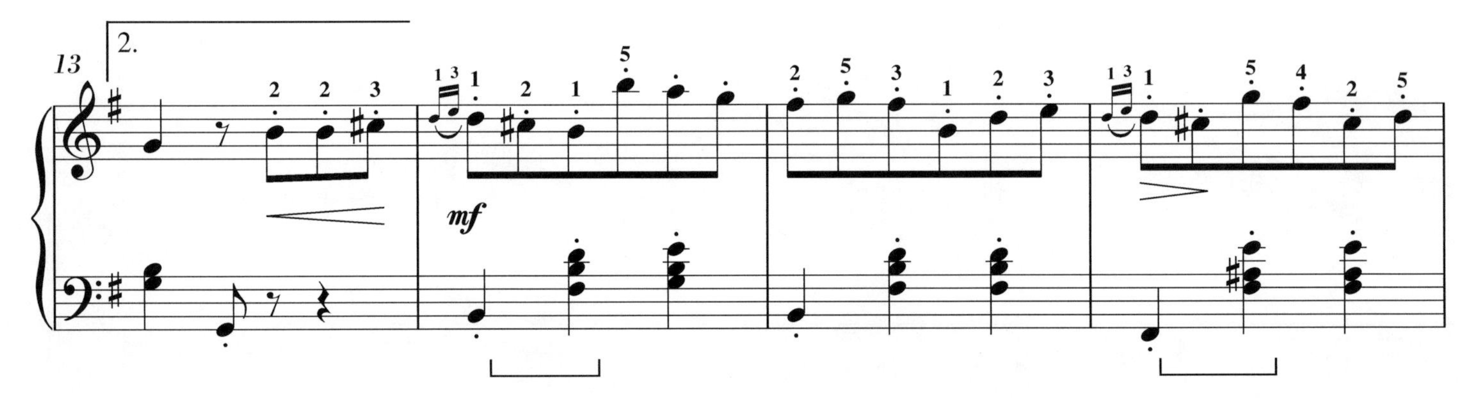

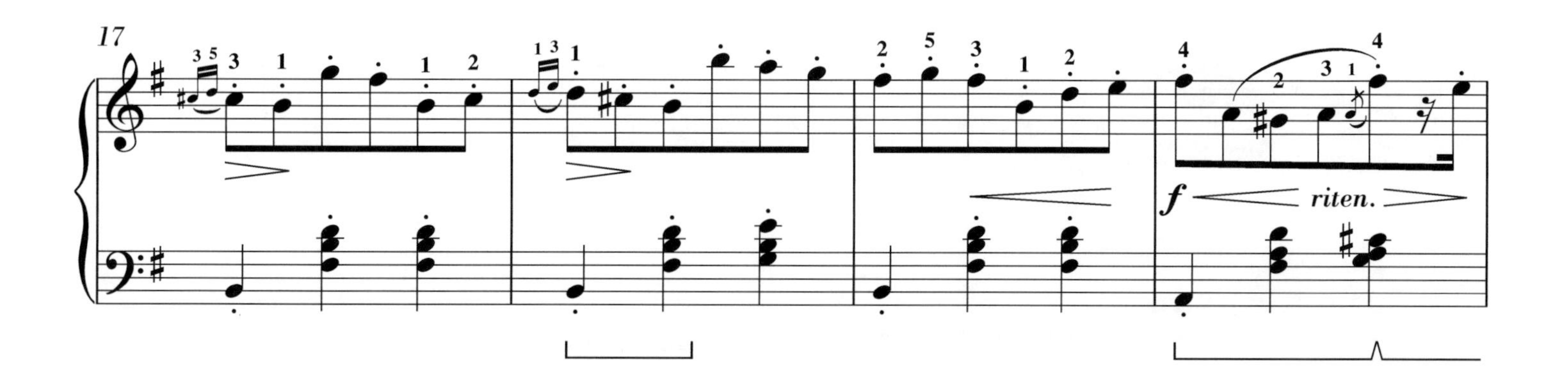
17
riten.

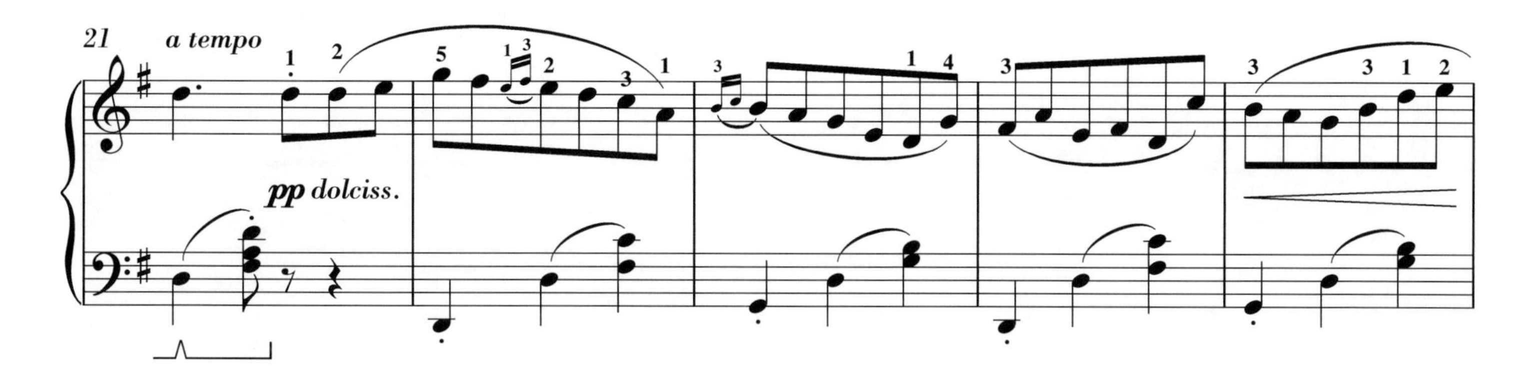
21
a tempo
pp dolciss.

26

30
f energico

34
dimin.
1.

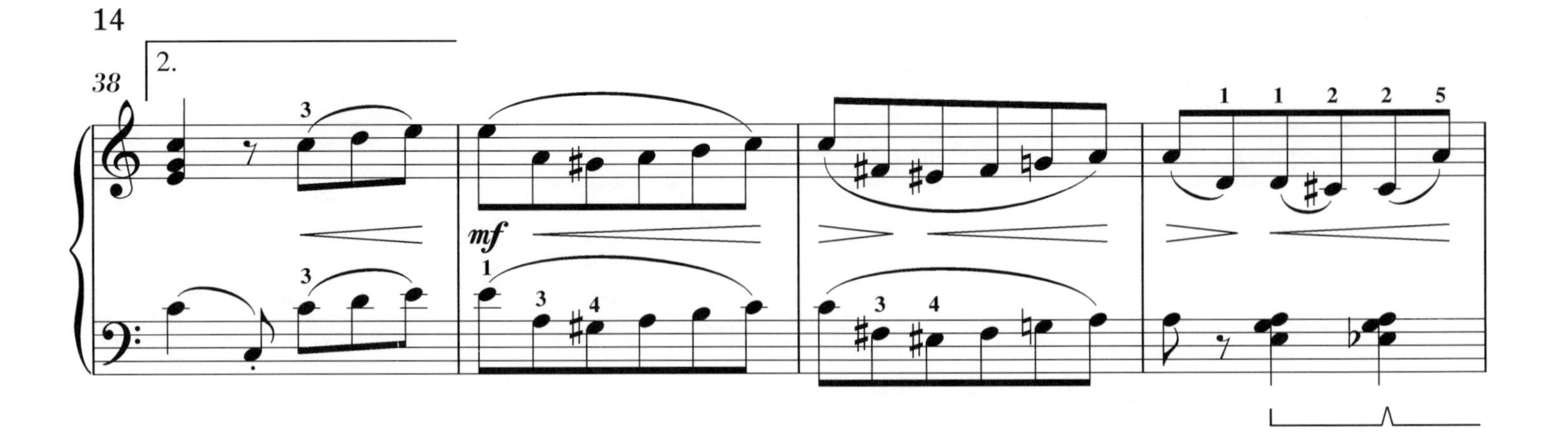
38
2.
mf

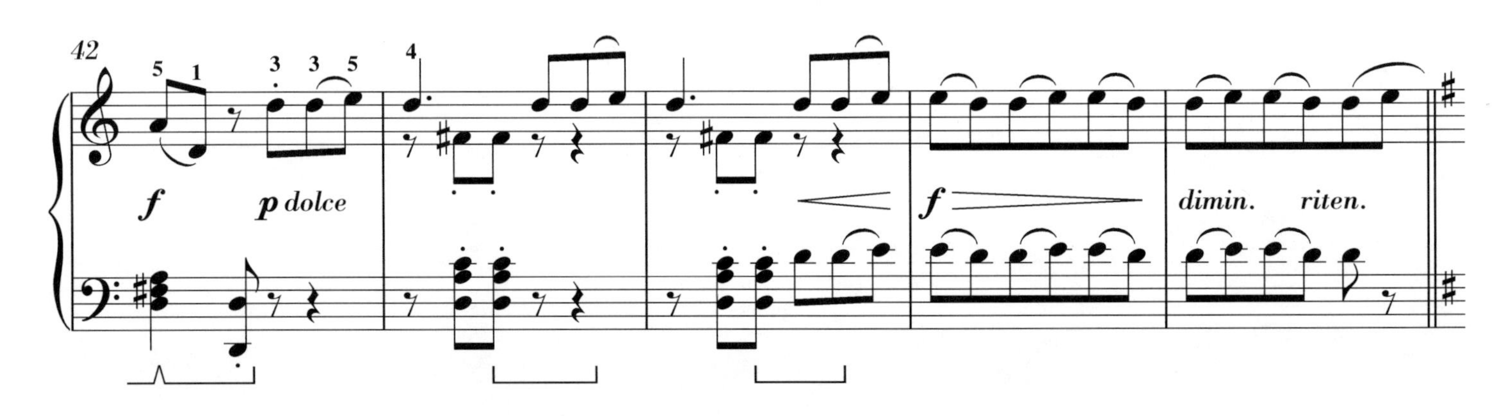
42
f
p dolce
f
dimin.
riten.

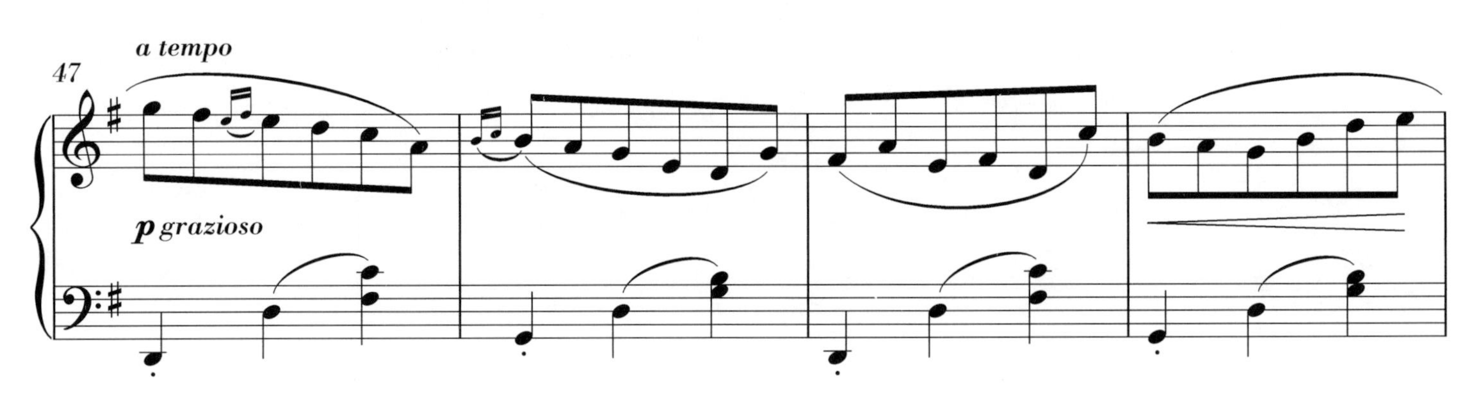
47
a tempo
p grazioso

51
sf
dimin.
p

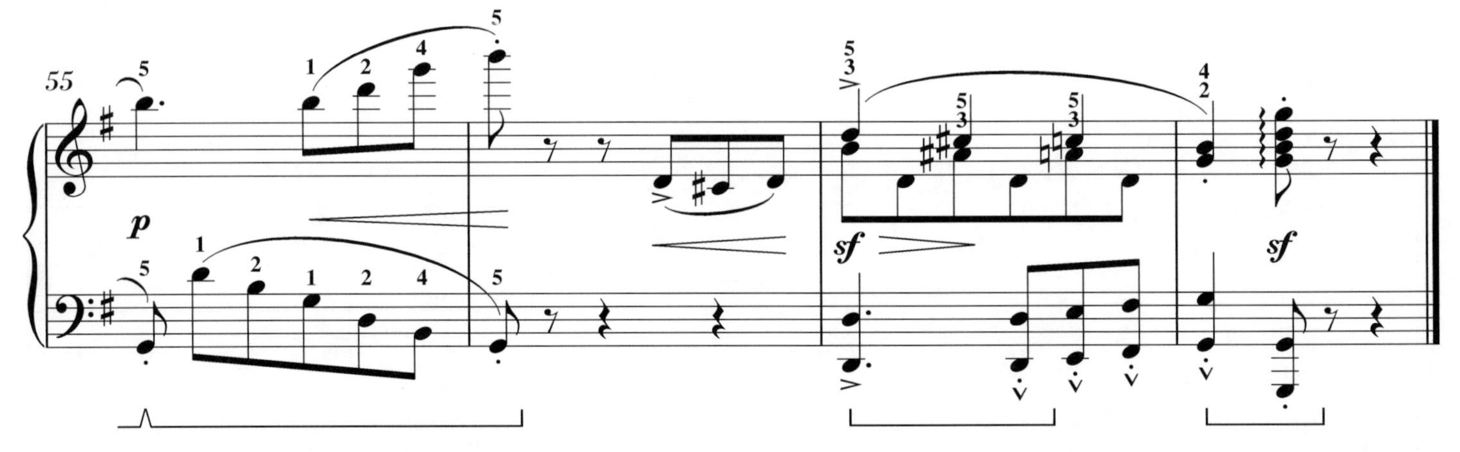
55
p
sf
sf

LABORUM
DULCE
LENIMEN
G. SCHIRMER

Les bohémiens

Gypsies

J. Friedrich Burgmüller
Op. 109, No. 4

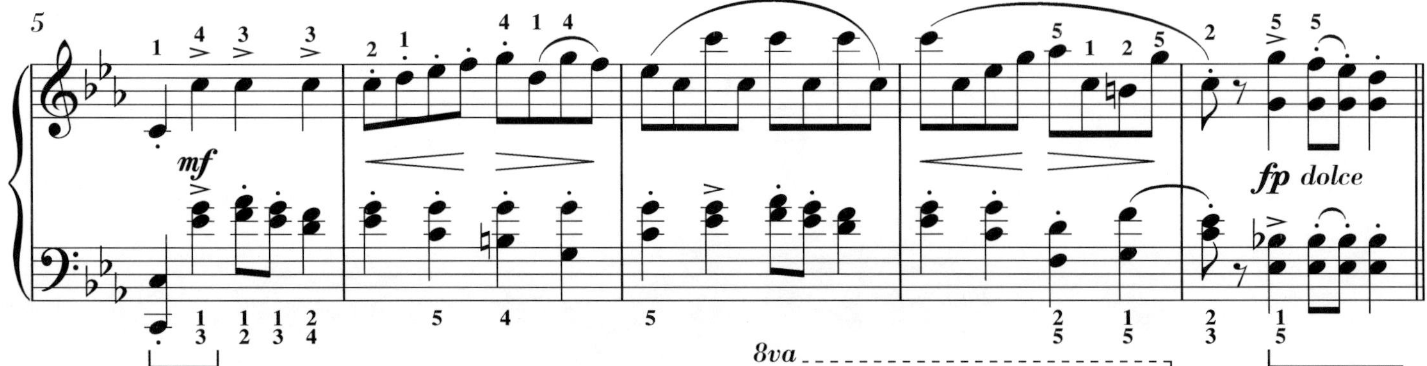

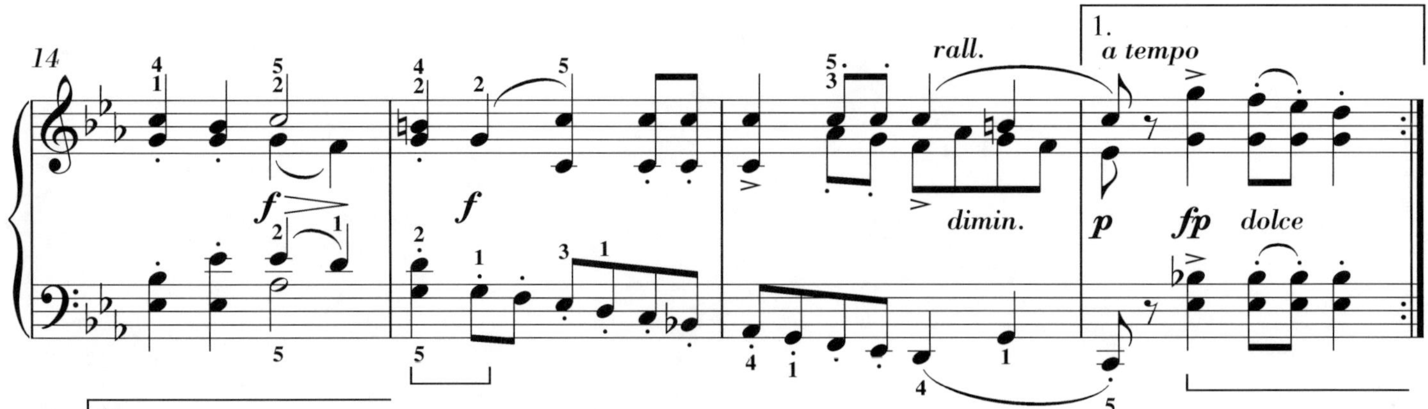

p legg.
p legg.

dimin.

cresc.

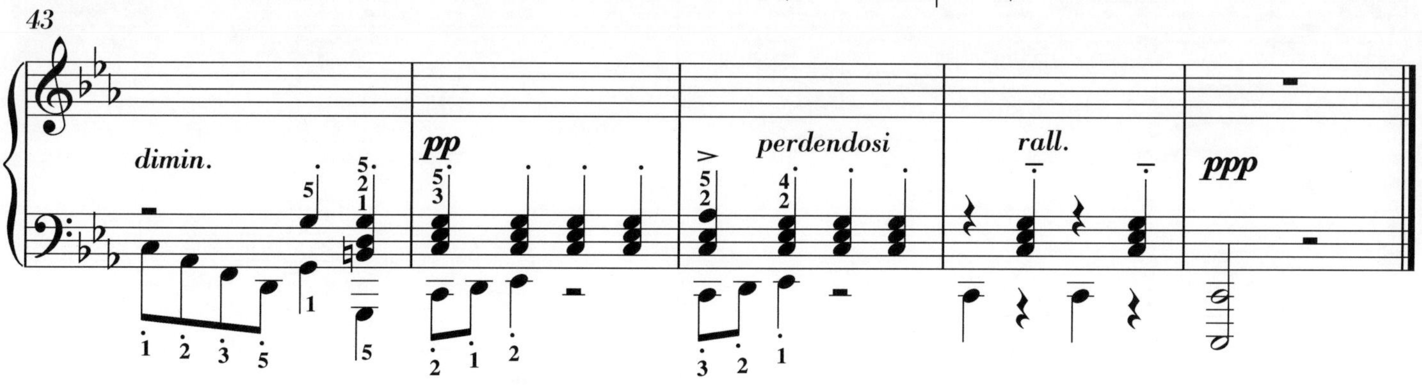
dimin.
perdendosi
rall.

La source

The Spring

J. Friedrich Burgmüller
Op. 109, No. 5

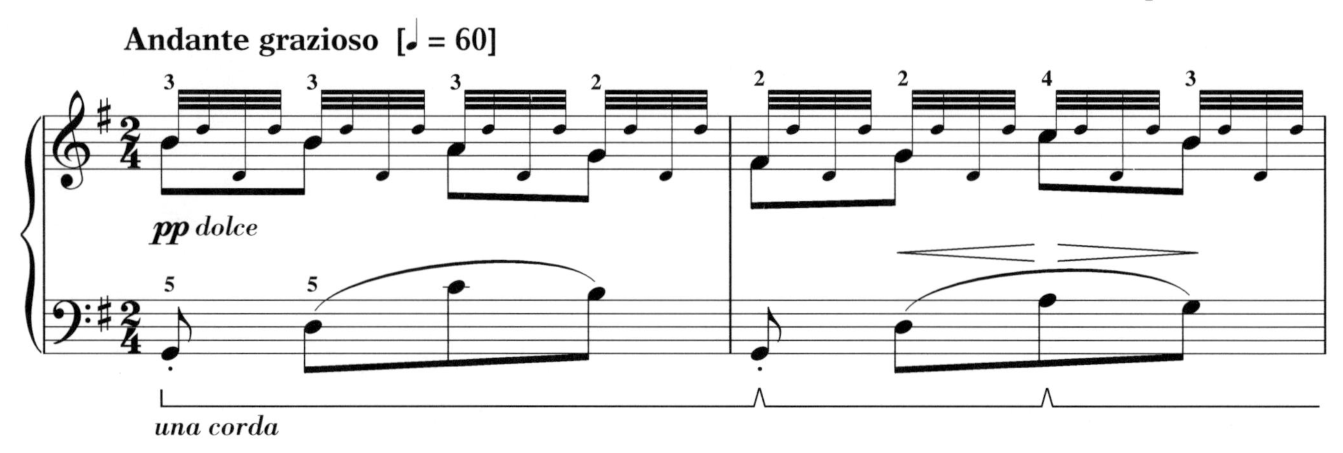

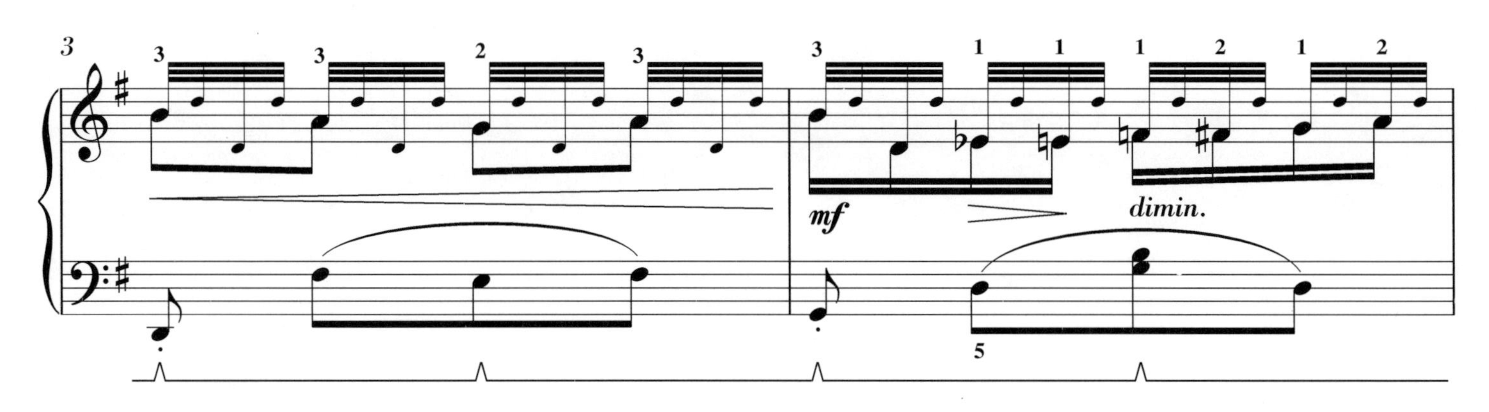

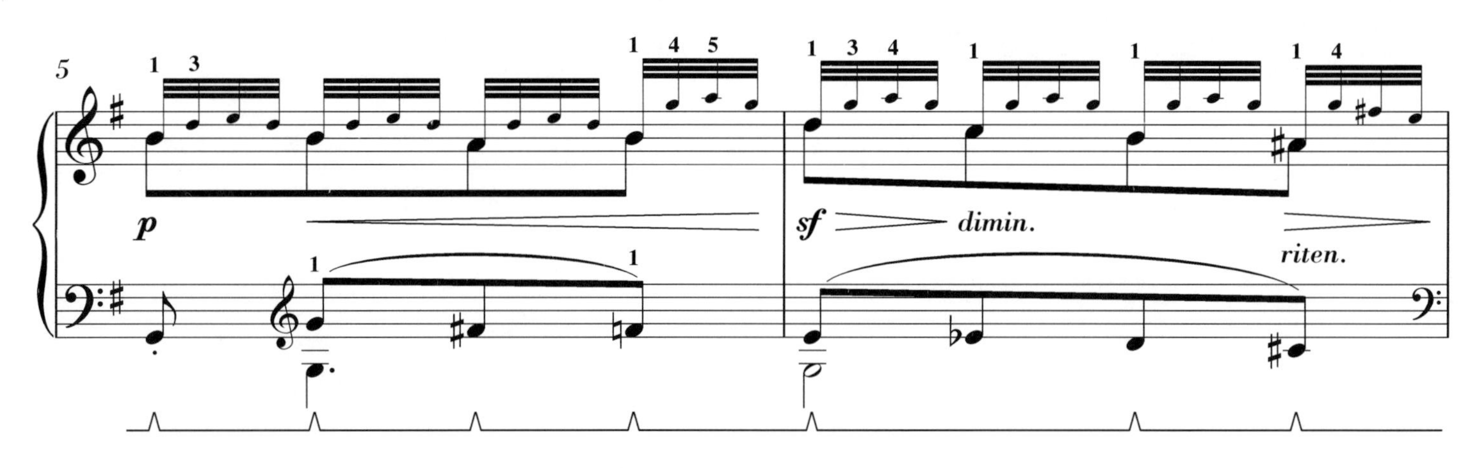

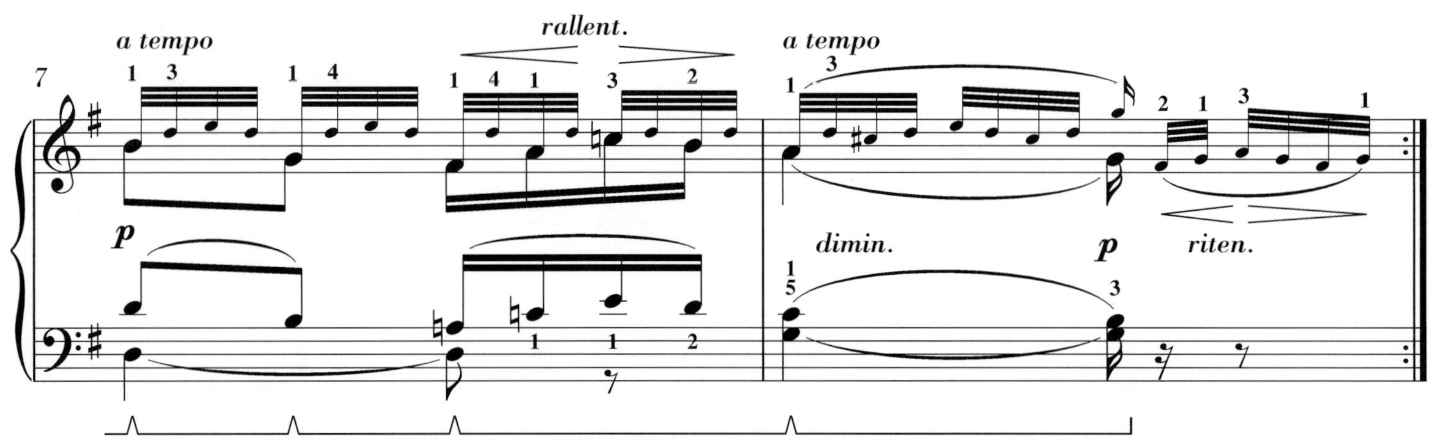

a tempo
9
mf

tre corde

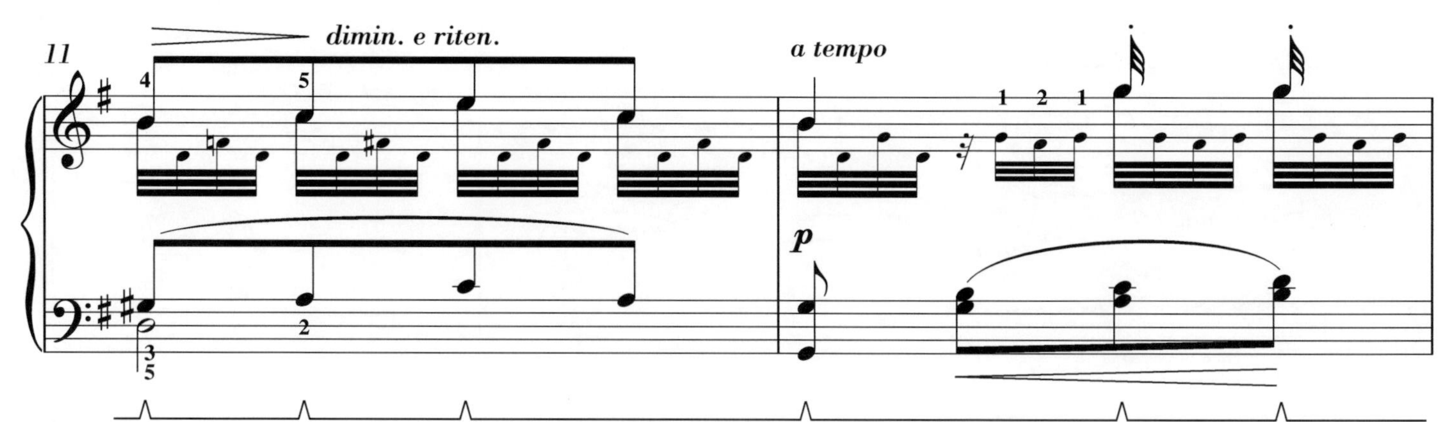
11
dimin. e riten.
a tempo
p

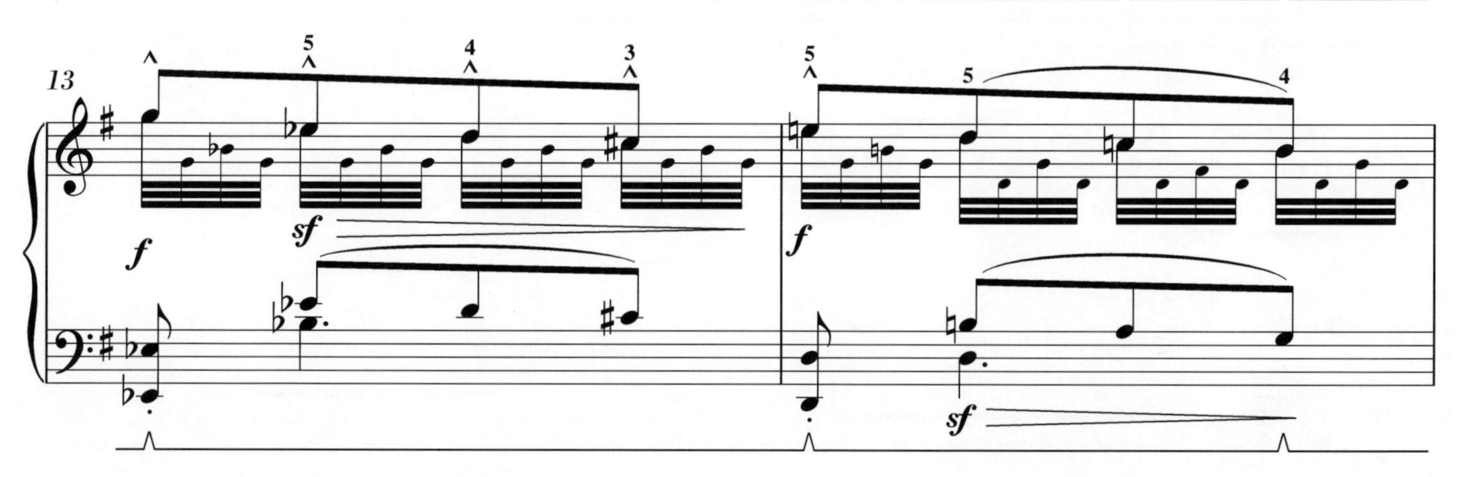
13
f
sf
15
dimin.
p
dimin. e ritard.

17
a tempo
pp dolce
una corda

20
mf
dimin.
p

22
a tempo
rall.
1.
a tempo
sf
dimin.
riten.
p
dimin.
p
riten.

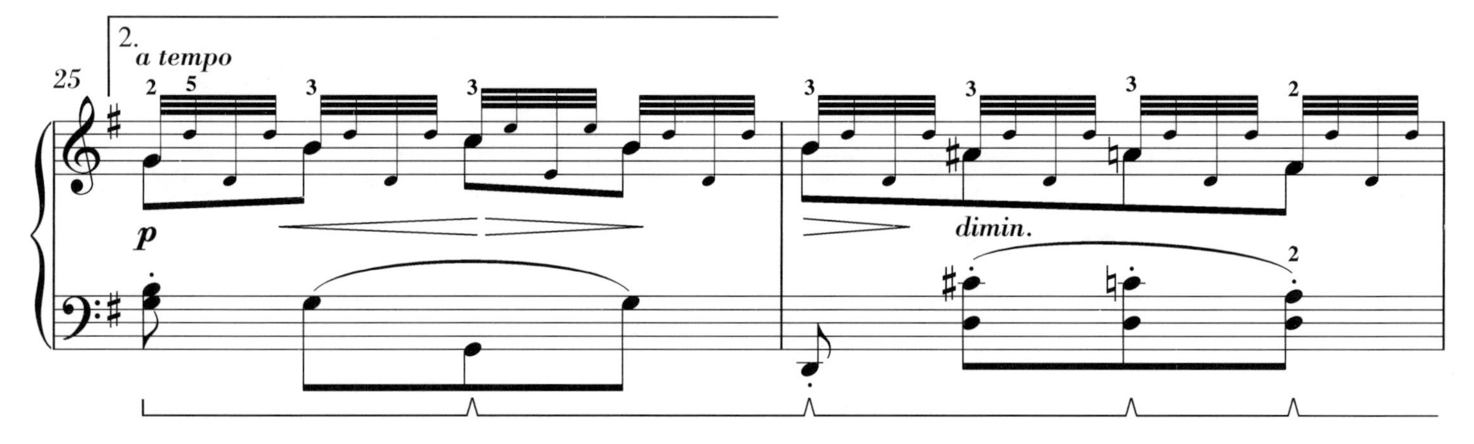
2.
a tempo
25
p
dimin.

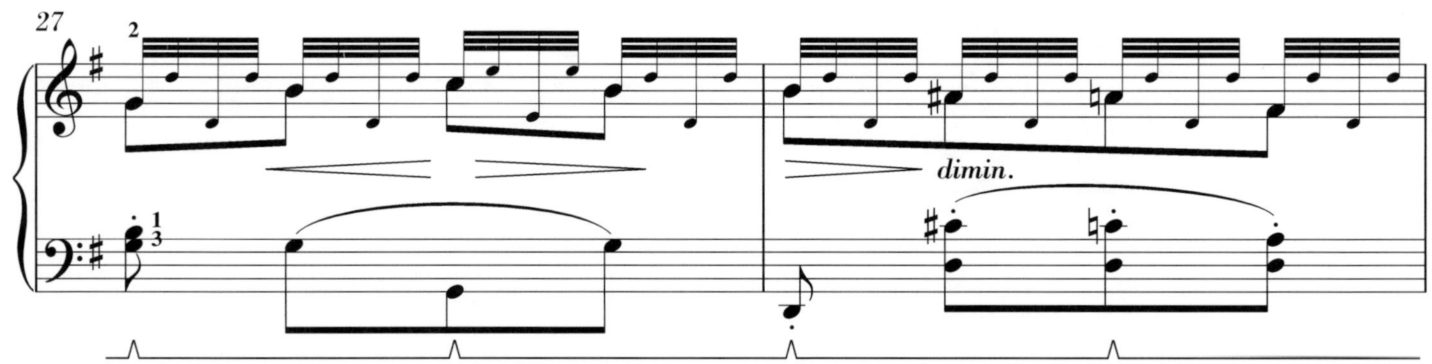
27
dimin.

29
p
dimin. e molto rall.
pp
dimin.
ppp

L'enjouée

The Light-hearted Lass

J. Friedrich Burgmüller
Op. 109, No. 6

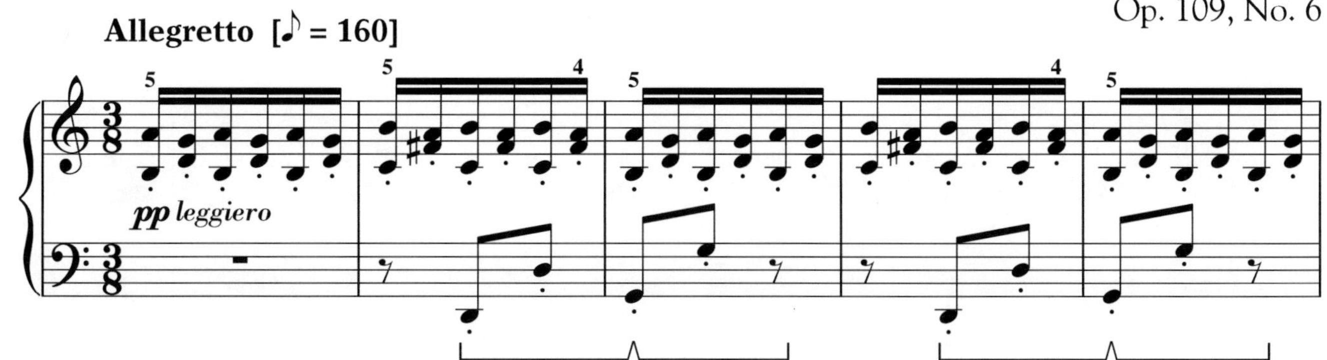

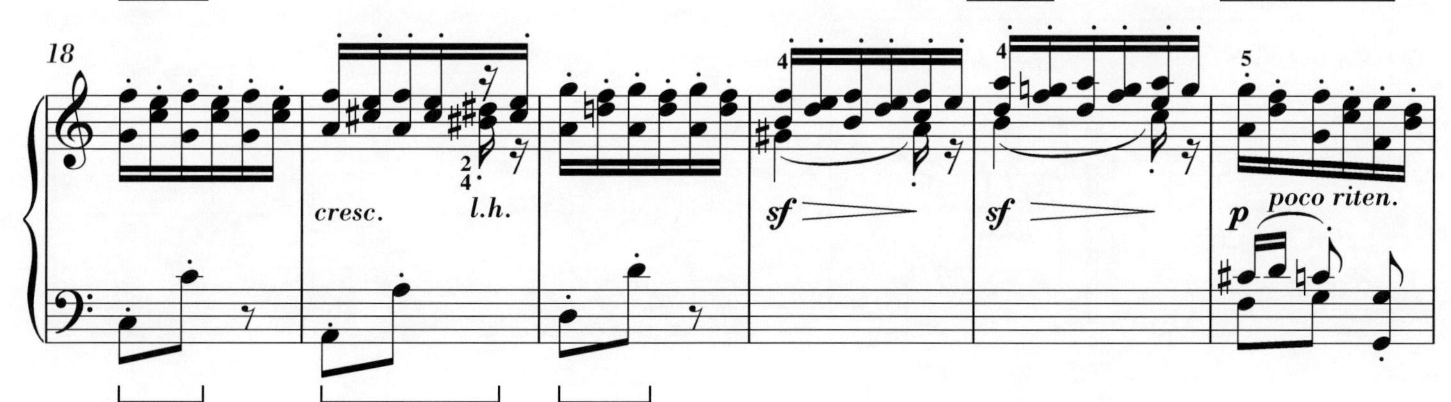

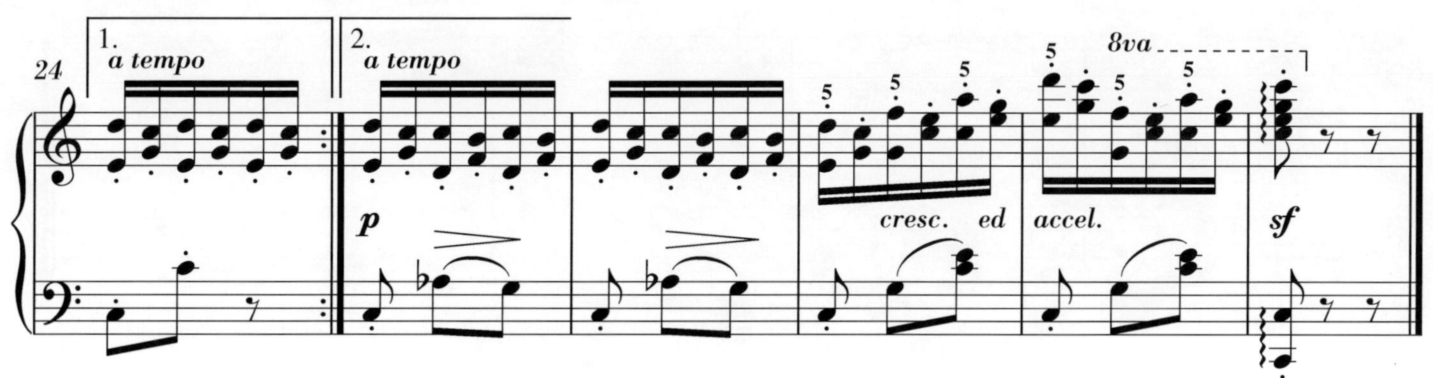

Berceuse

Lullaby

J. Friedrich Burgmüller
Op. 109, No. 7

Andantino con moto [♪ = 120]

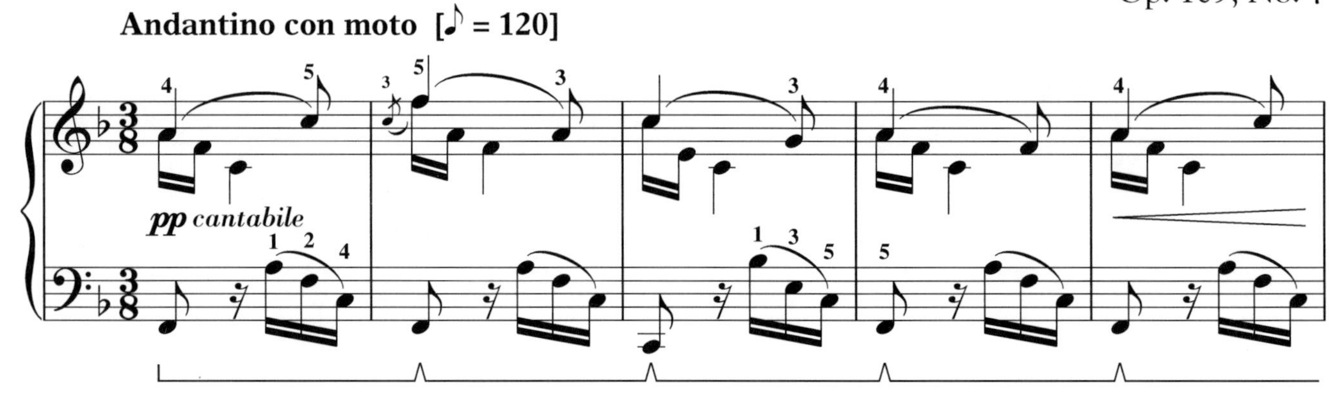

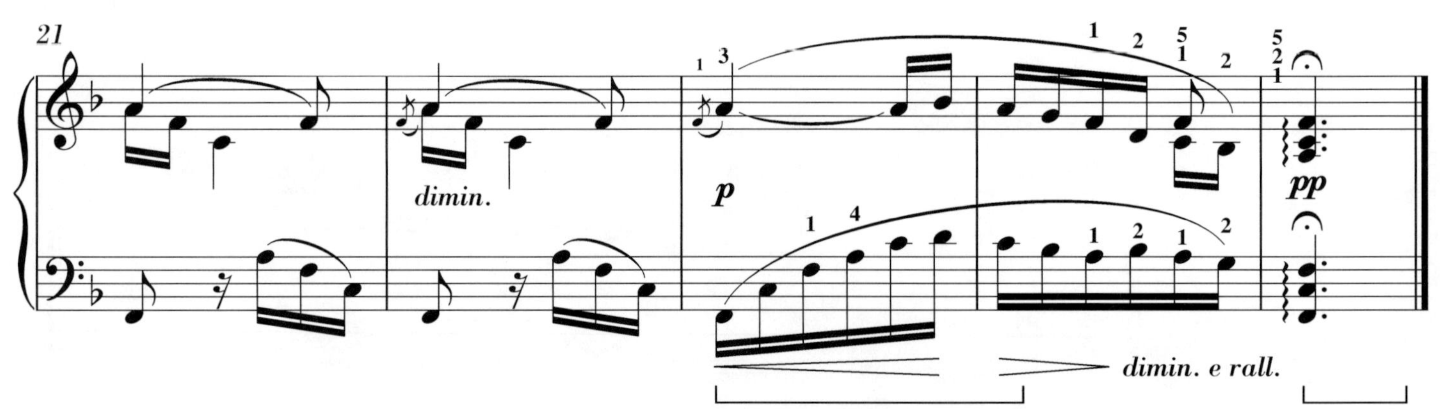

Agitato

J. Friedrich Burgmüller
Op. 109, No. 8

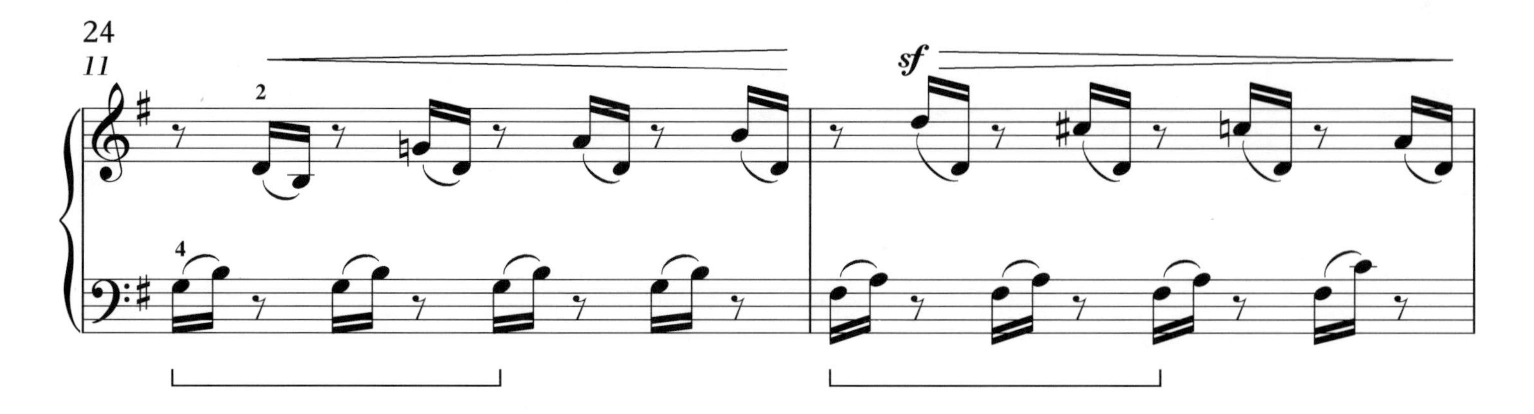
11
sf

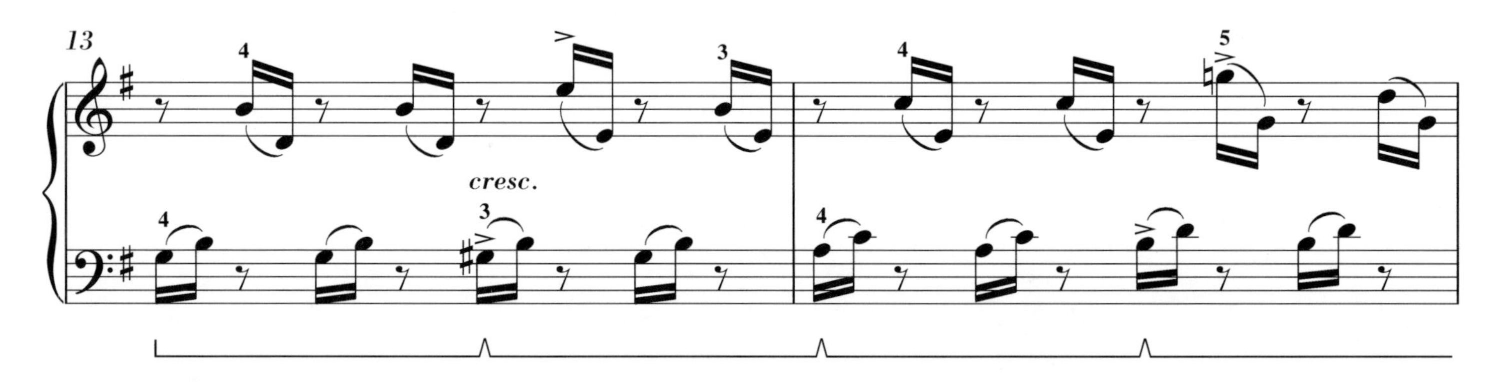
13
cresc.

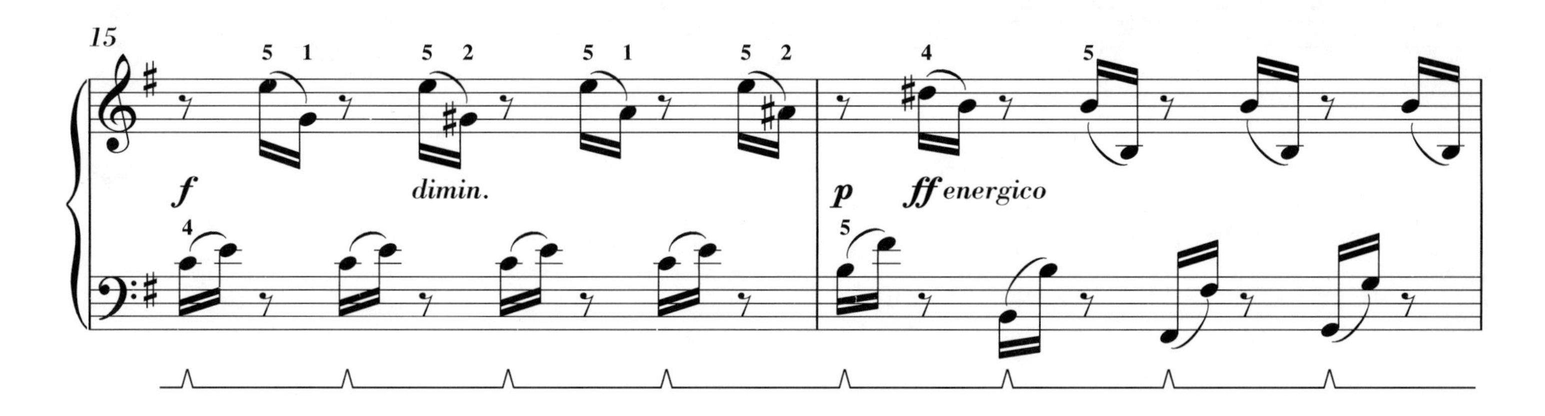
15
f
dimin.
p
ff energico

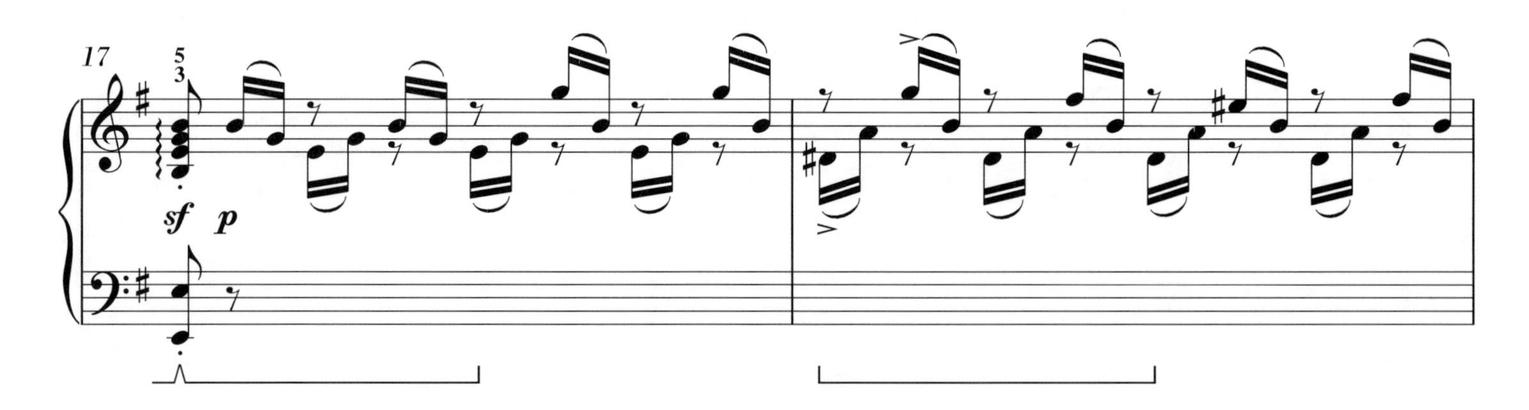
17
sf
p

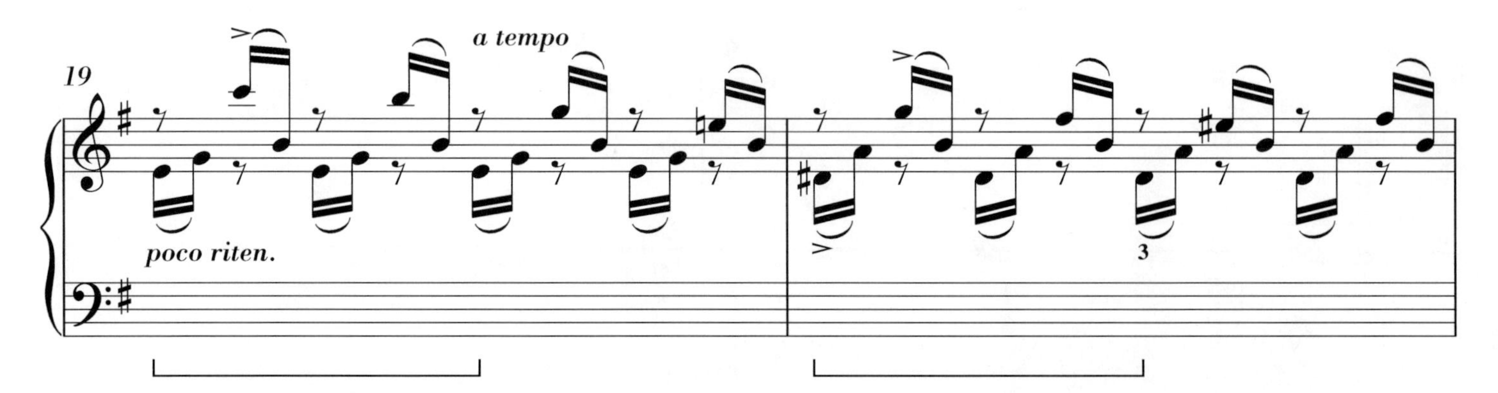
19
a tempo
poco riten.

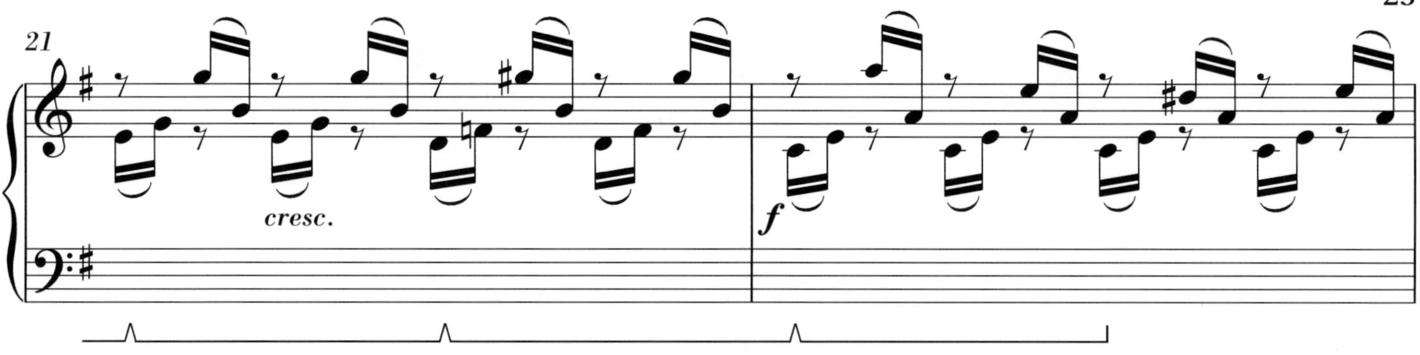
21
cresc.
f

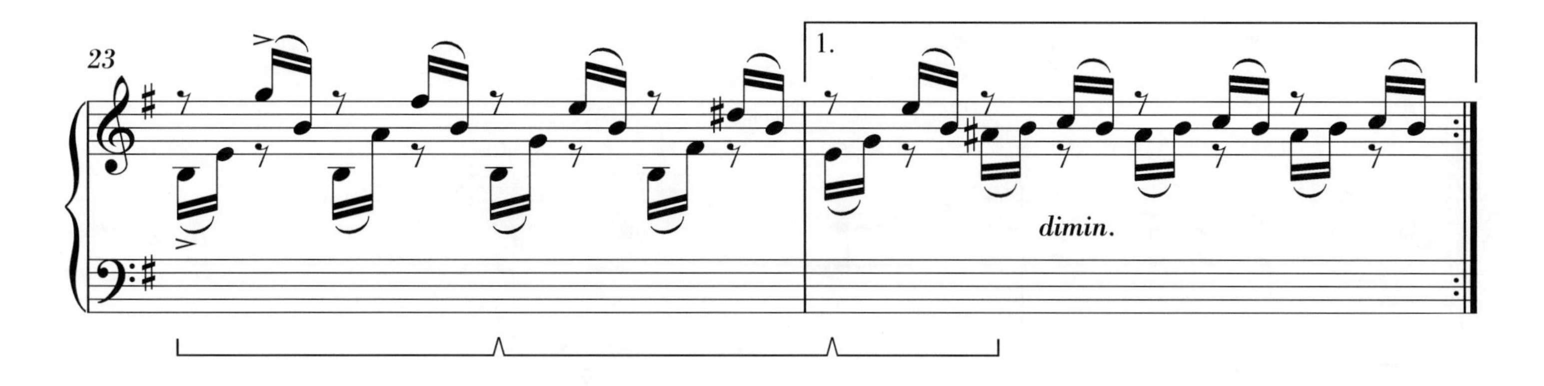
23
1.
dimin.

25
2.
p

27
cresc. ed accel.

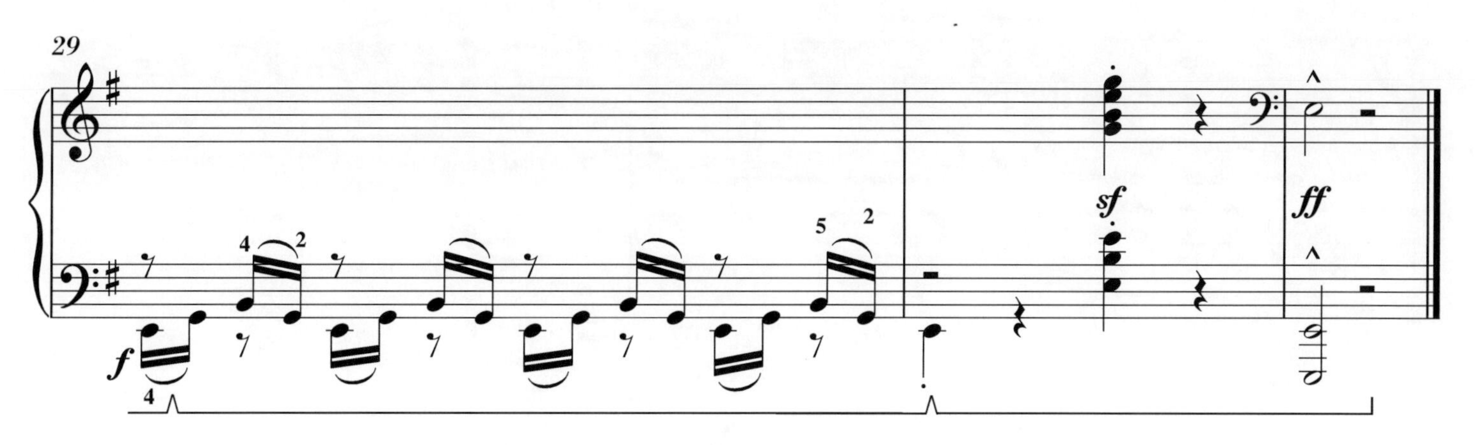
29
f
sf
ff

La cloche des matines

The Matin Bell

J. Friedrich Burgmüller
Op. 109, No. 9

Andante sostenuto [♩ = 92]

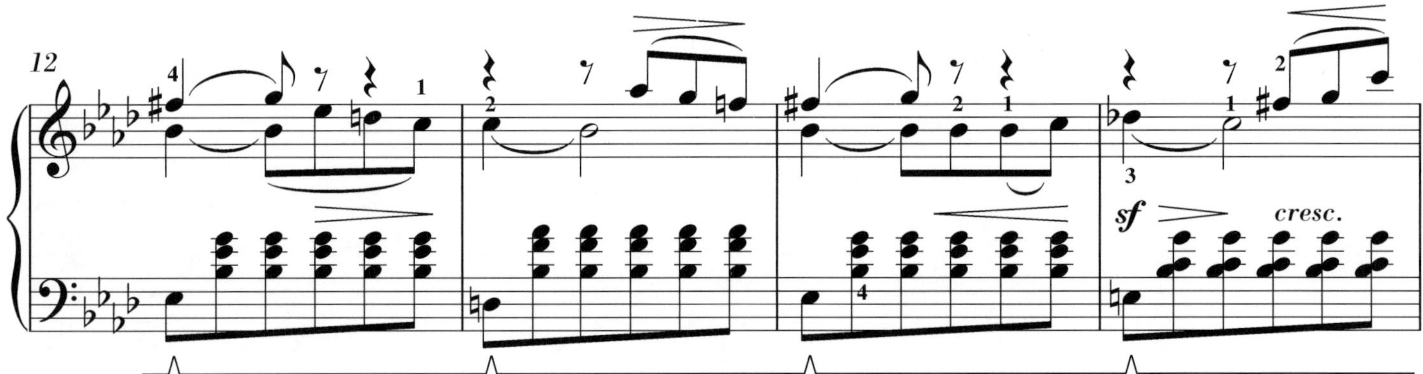

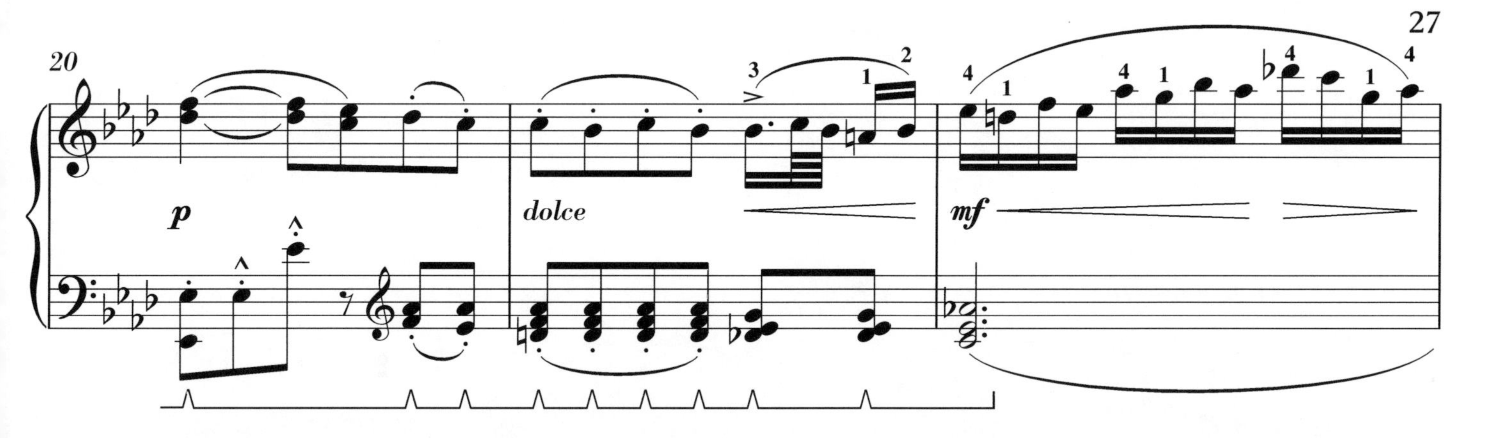
20
p
dolce
mf

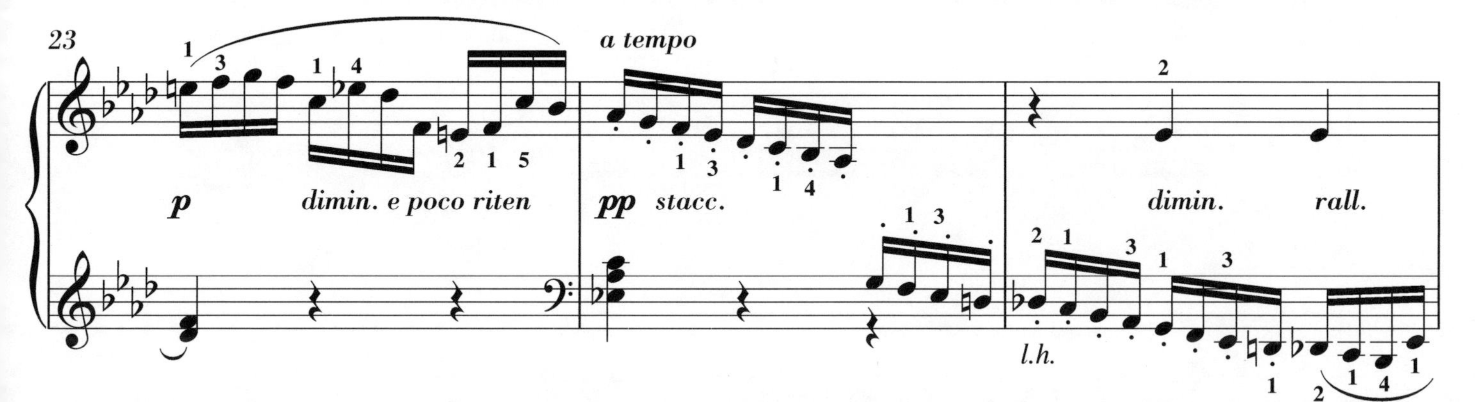
23
a tempo
p
dimin. e poco riten
pp
stacc.
dimin.
rall.
l.h.

26
a tempo

30
sf
sf
p
dimin.

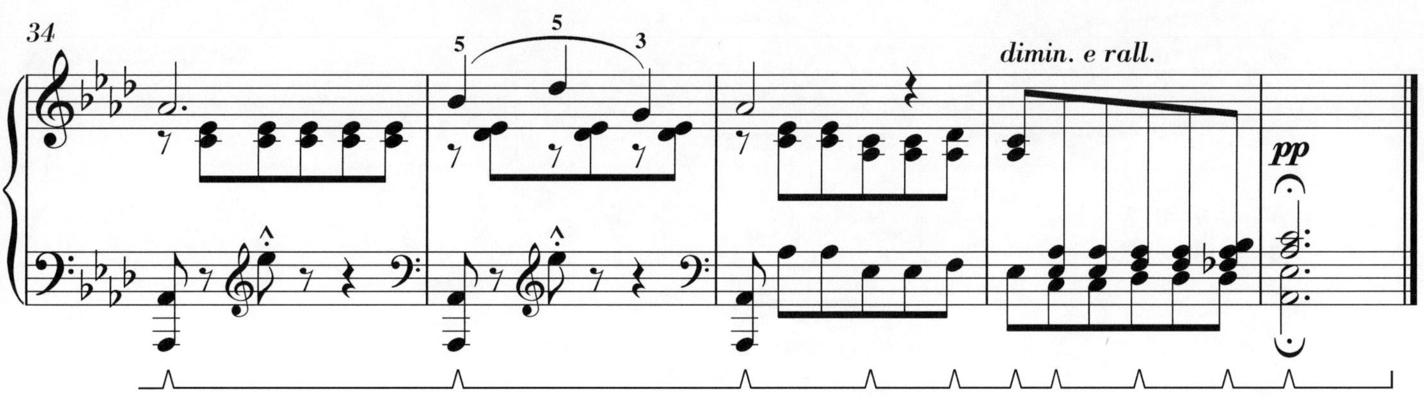
34
dimin. e rall.
pp

La vélocité

Velocity

J. Friedrich Burgmüller

Op. 109, No. 10

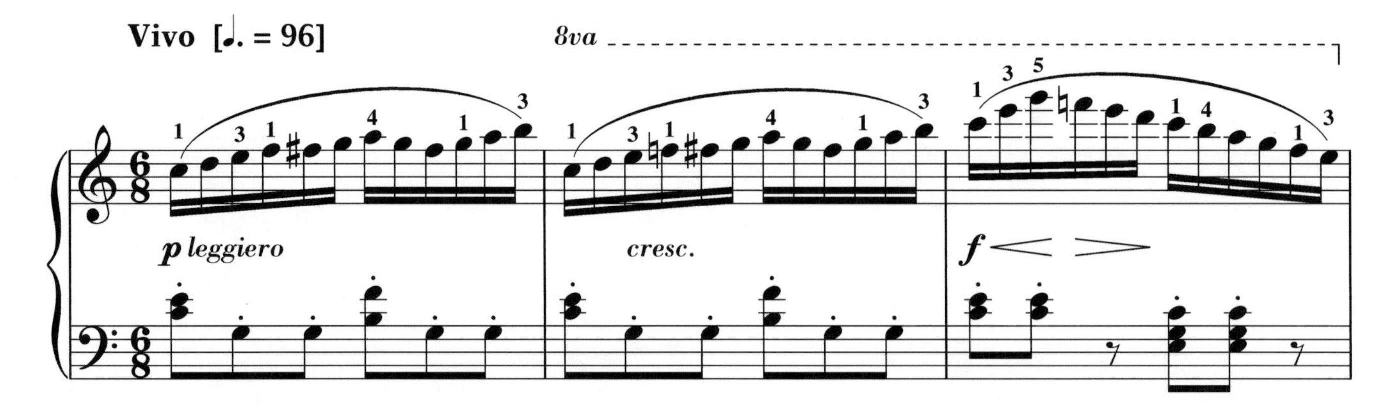

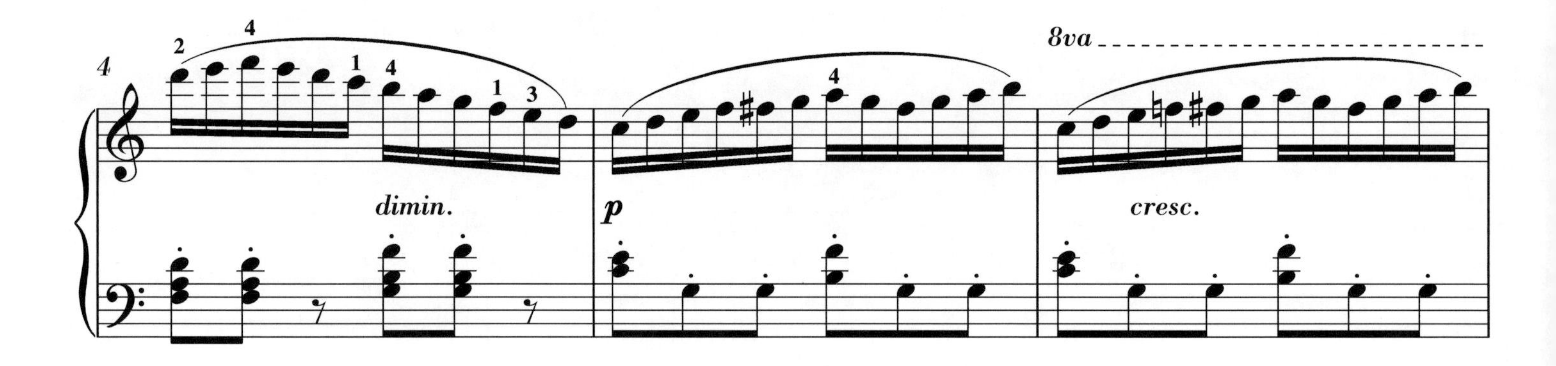

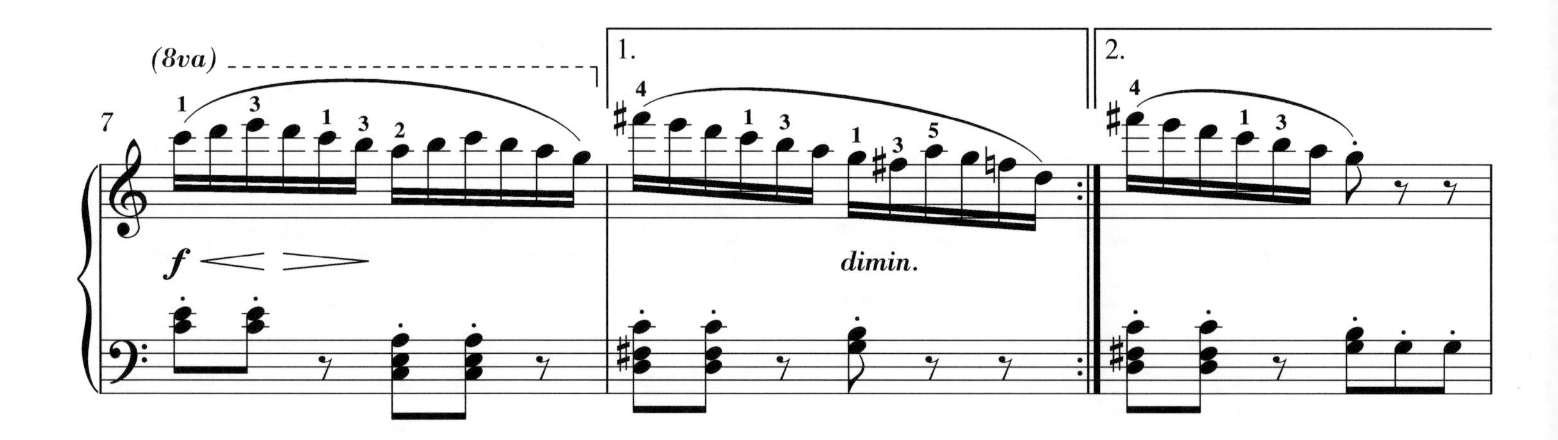

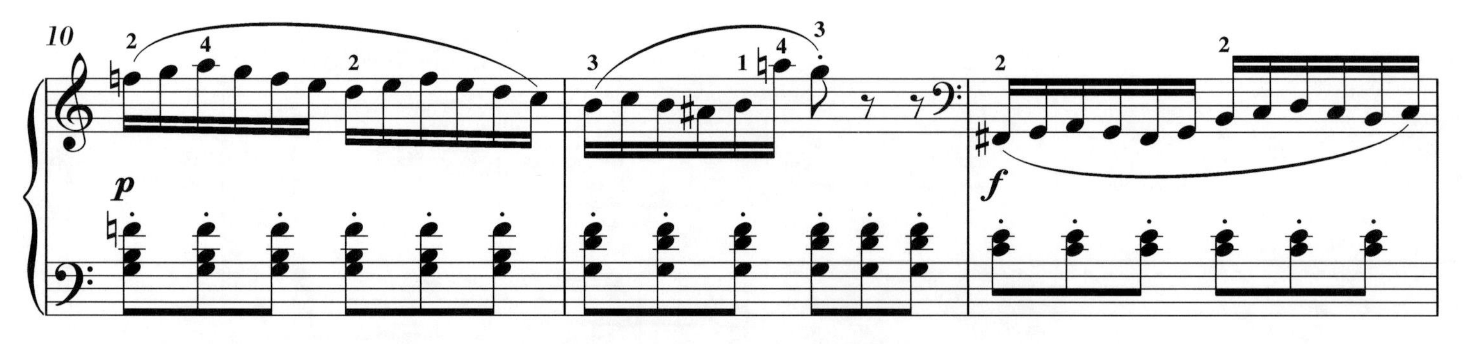

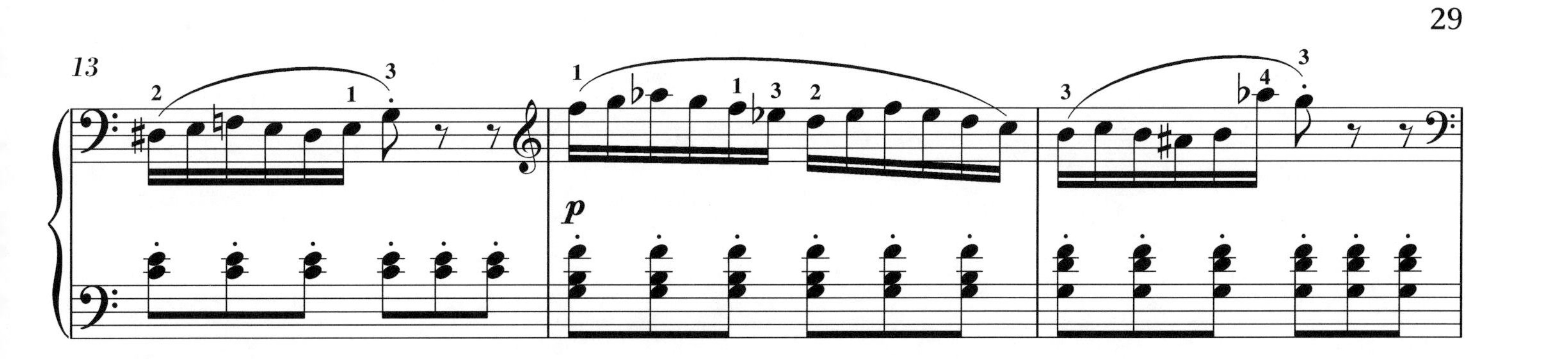
13
p

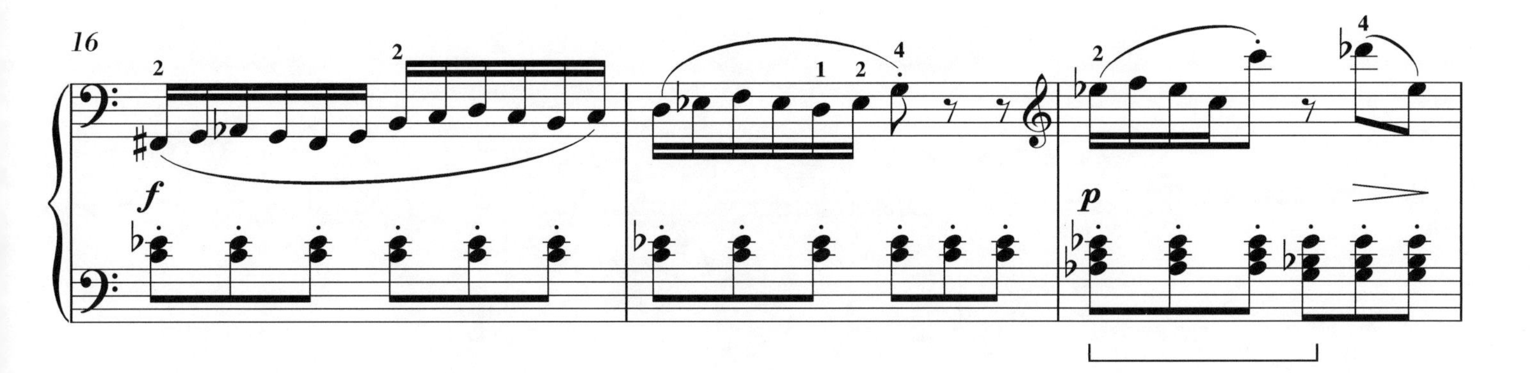
16
f
p

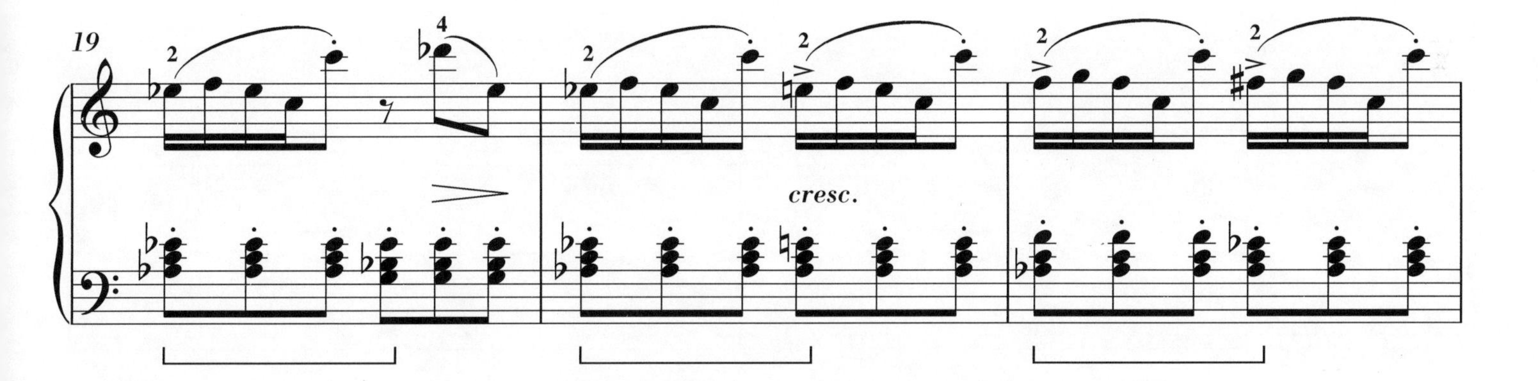
19
cresc.

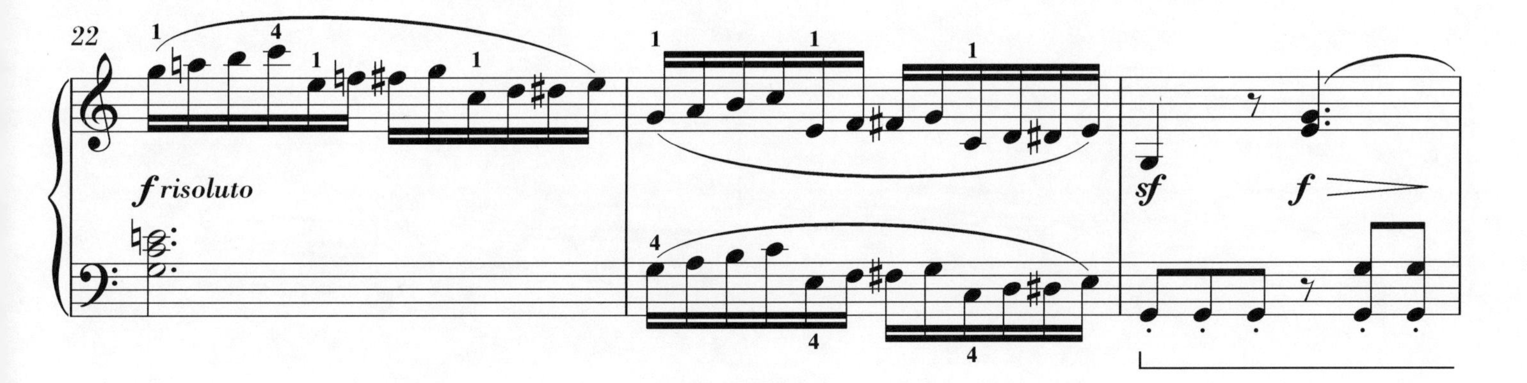
22
f risoluto
sf
f

8va
25
a tempo
dimin. e rall.
p
cresc.

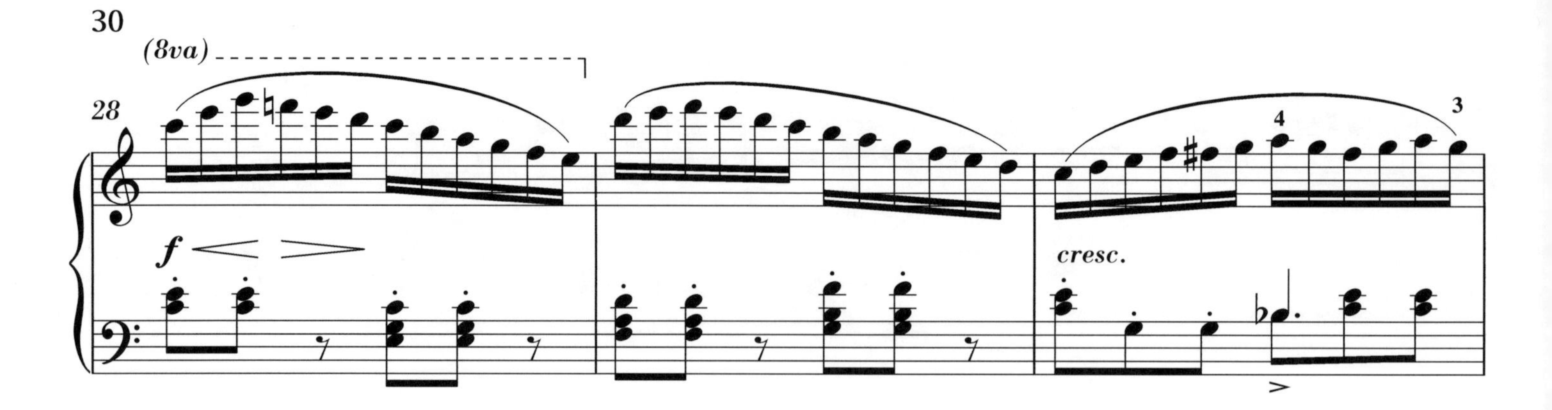
(8va)
28
f
cresc.

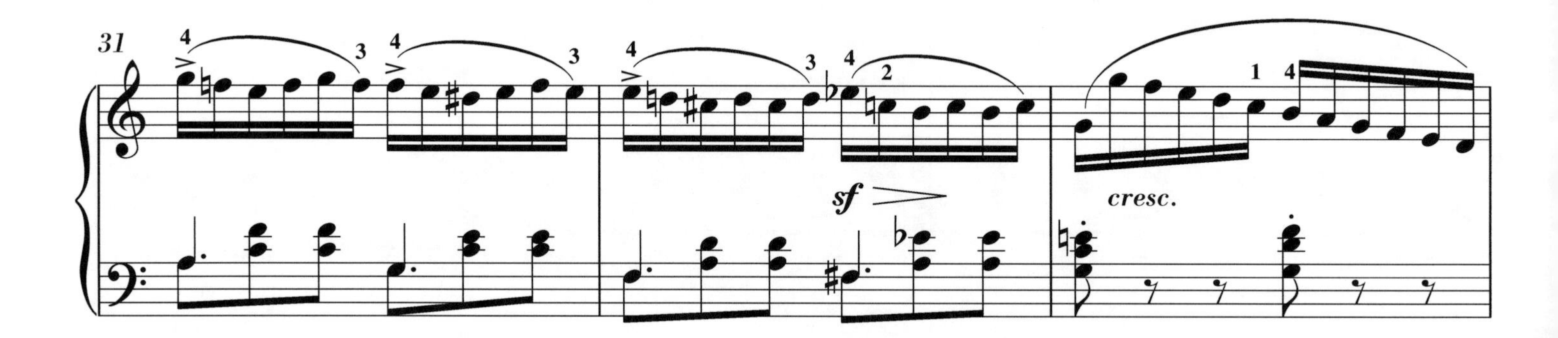
31
sf
cresc.

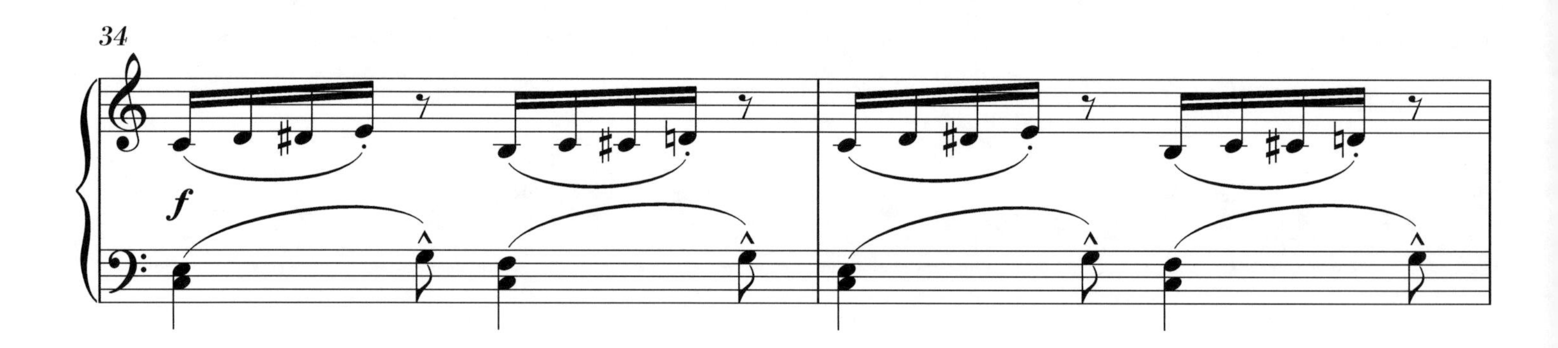
34
f

36
r.h.

38
sf
sf
sf
sf

La sérénade

Serenade

J. Friedrich Burgmüller
Op. 109, No. 11

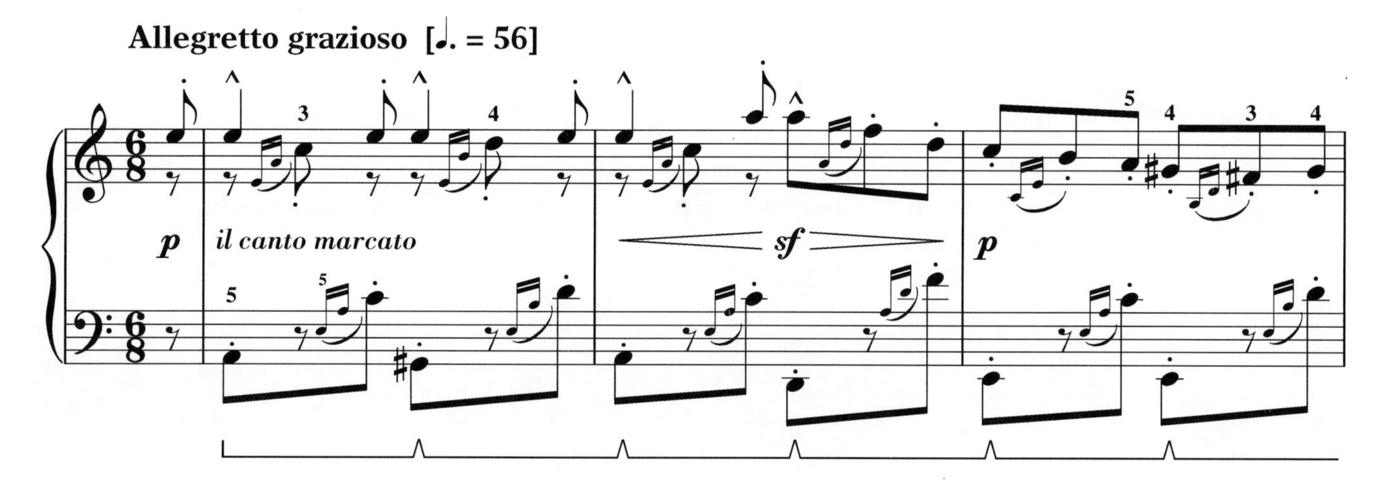

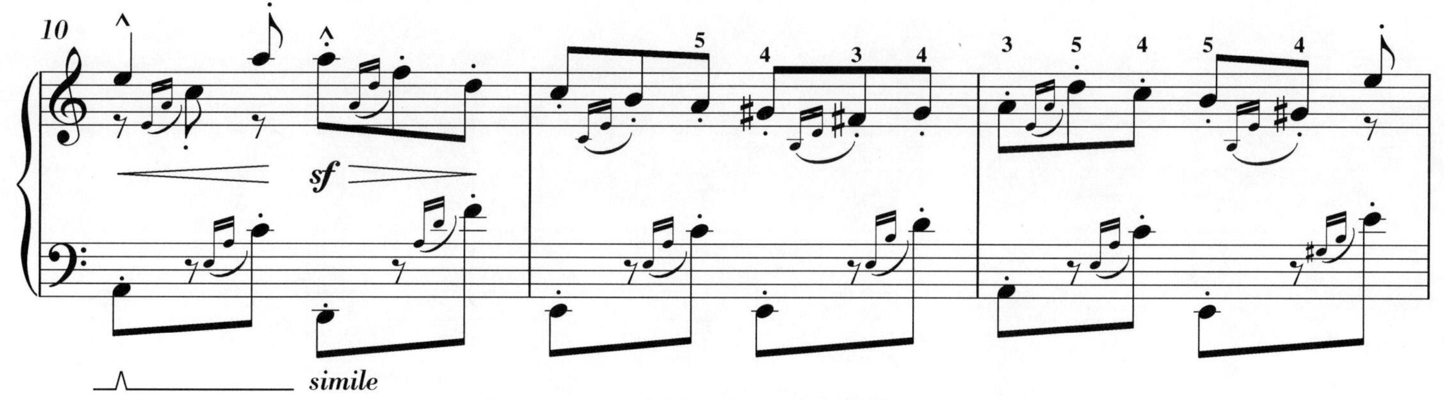

13
cresc.
f
dimin. e poco riten.

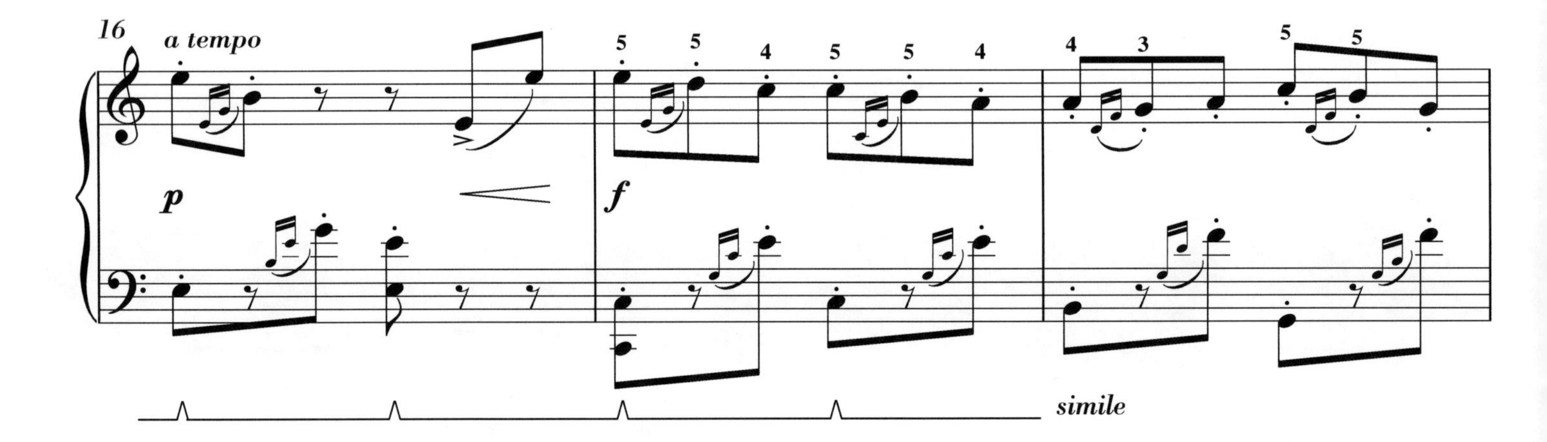
16
a tempo
p
f
simile

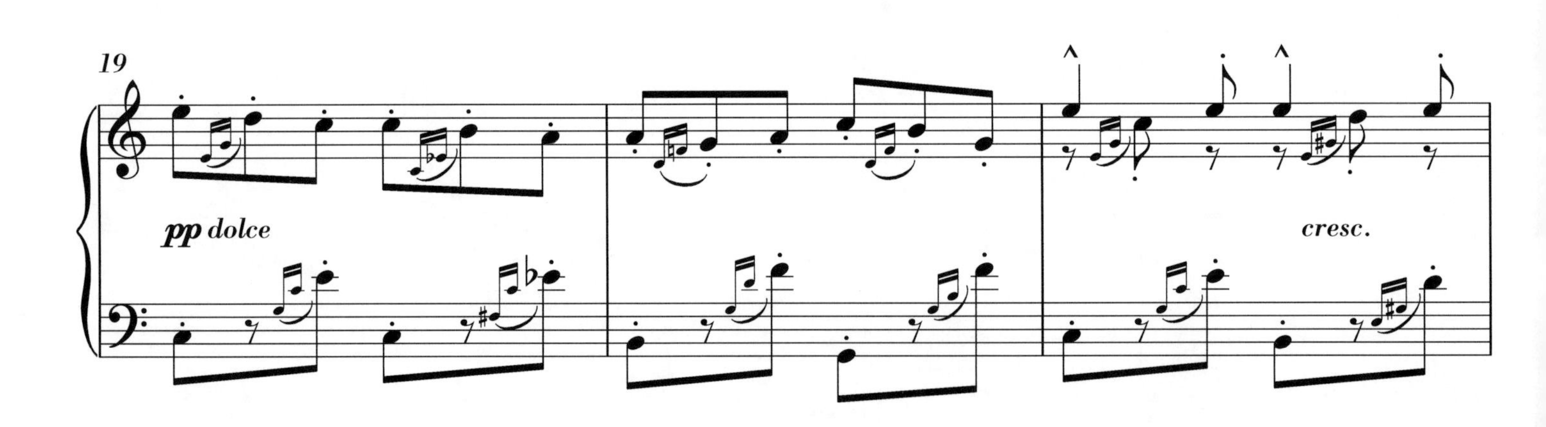
19
pp dolce
cresc.

22
sf
dimin.

25
f
pp dolce
simile

28
cresc.
sf

31
dimin.

34

36
perdendosi e sempre più ritenuto
pp

Le réveil dans les bois

Awakening in the Woods

J. Friedrich Burgmüller
Op. 109, No. 12

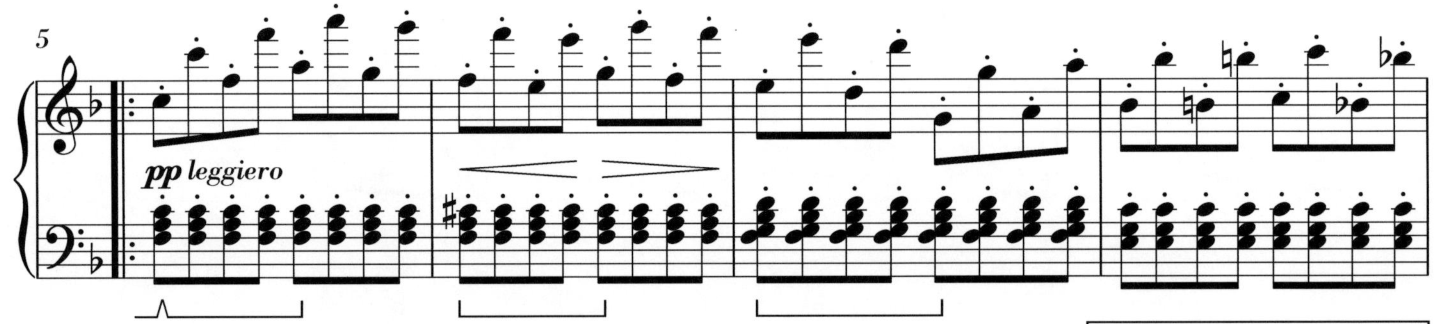

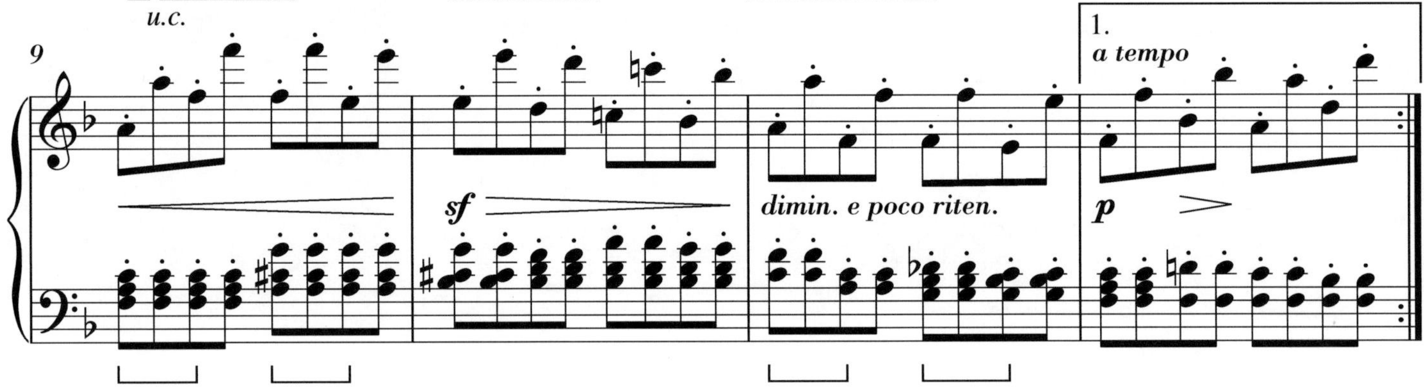

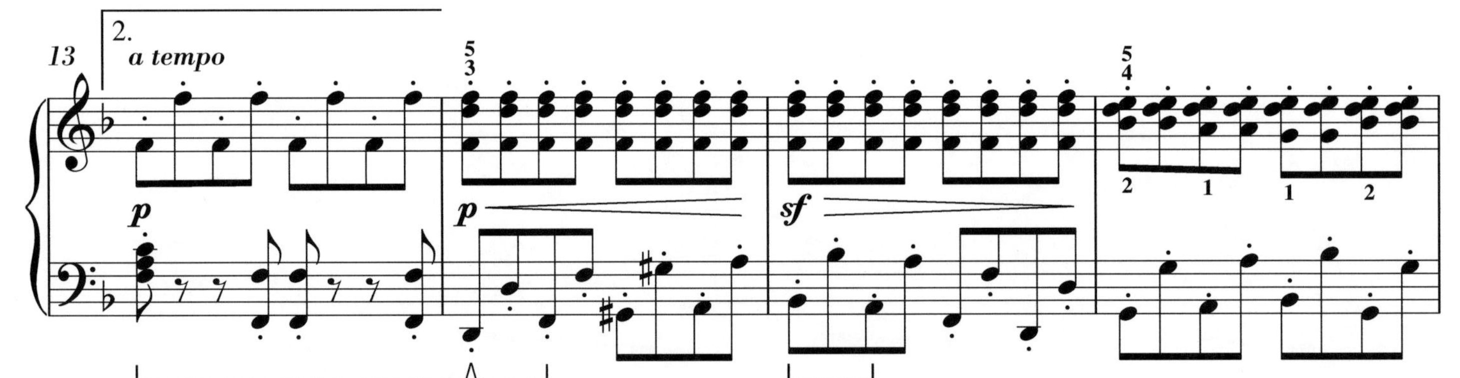

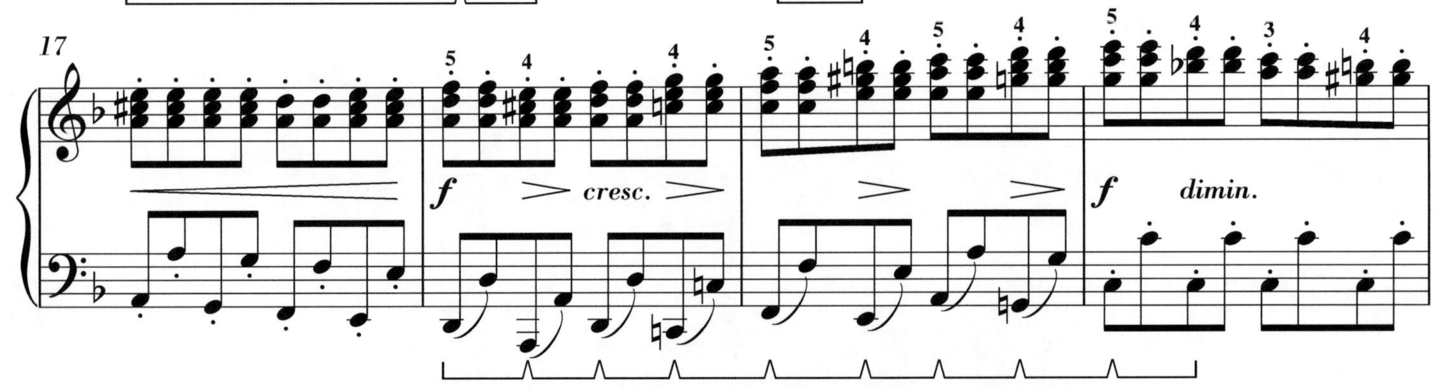

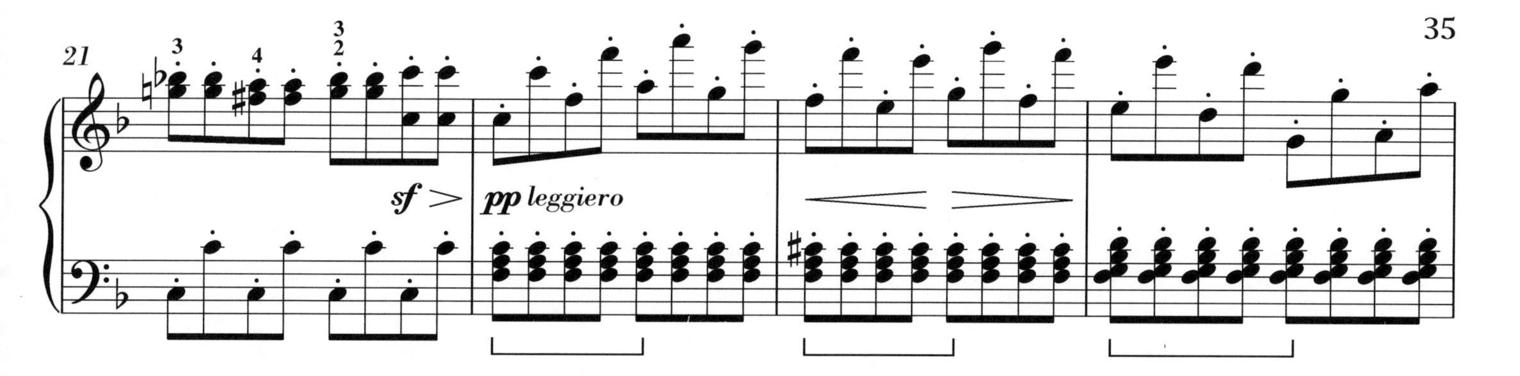
21
sf
pp leggiero

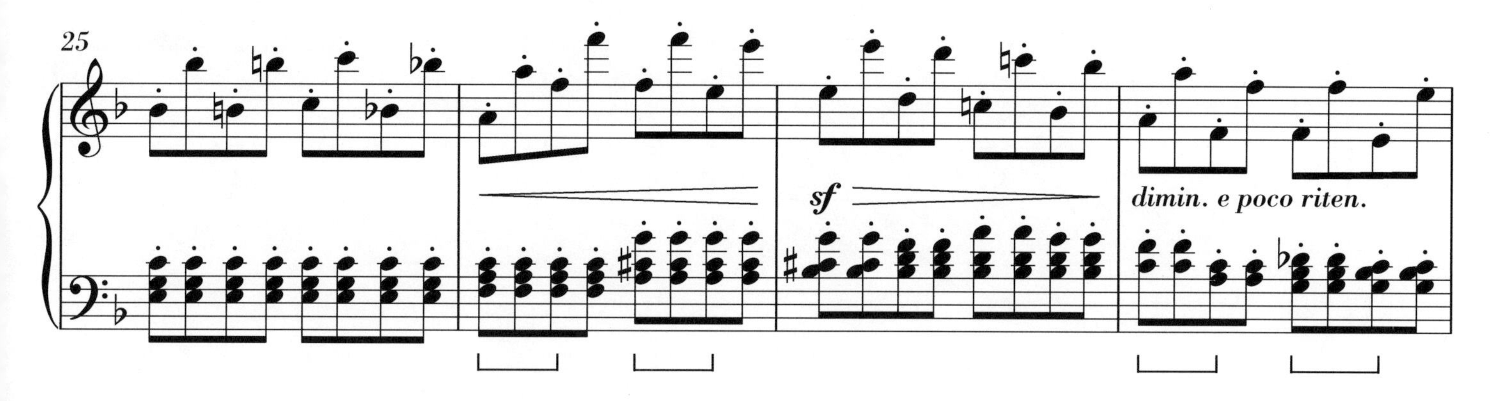
25
sf
dimin. e poco riten.

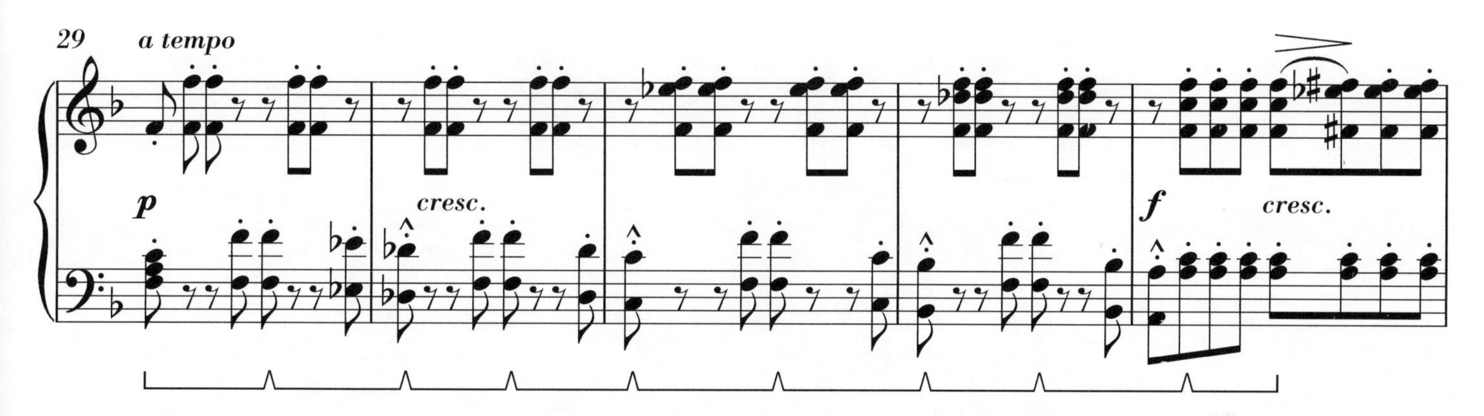
29
a tempo
p
cresc.
f
cresc.

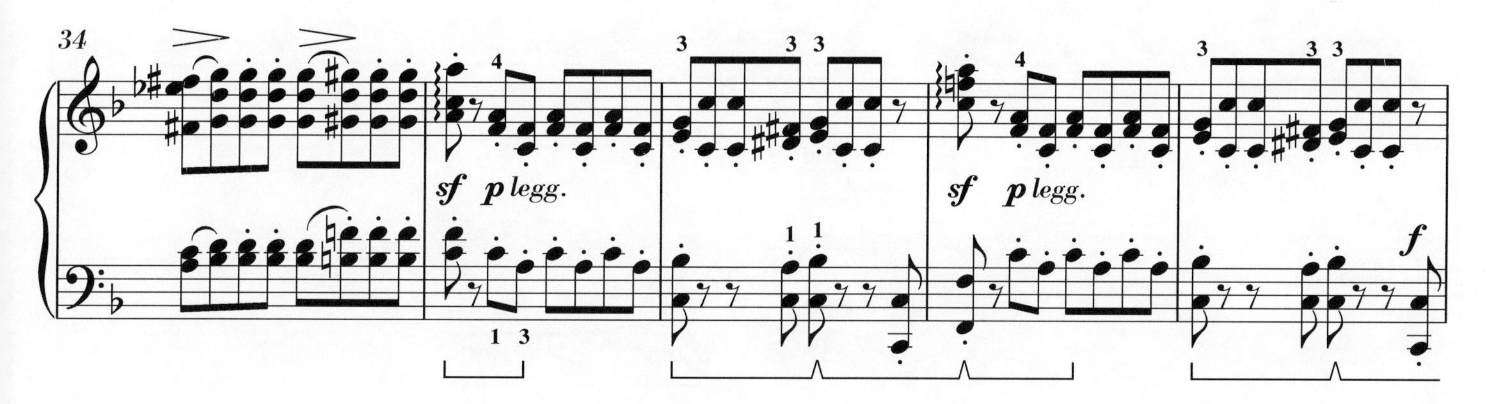
34
sf
p legg.
sf
p legg.
f

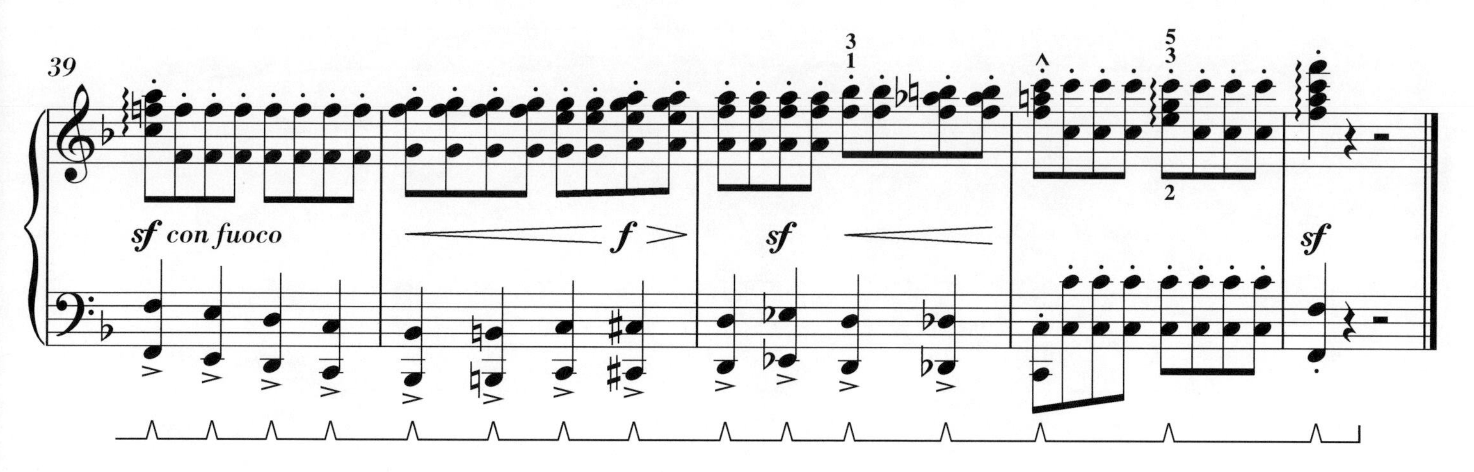
39
sf con fuoco
f
sf
sf

L'orage
The Storm

J. Friedrich Burgmüller
Op. 109, No. 13

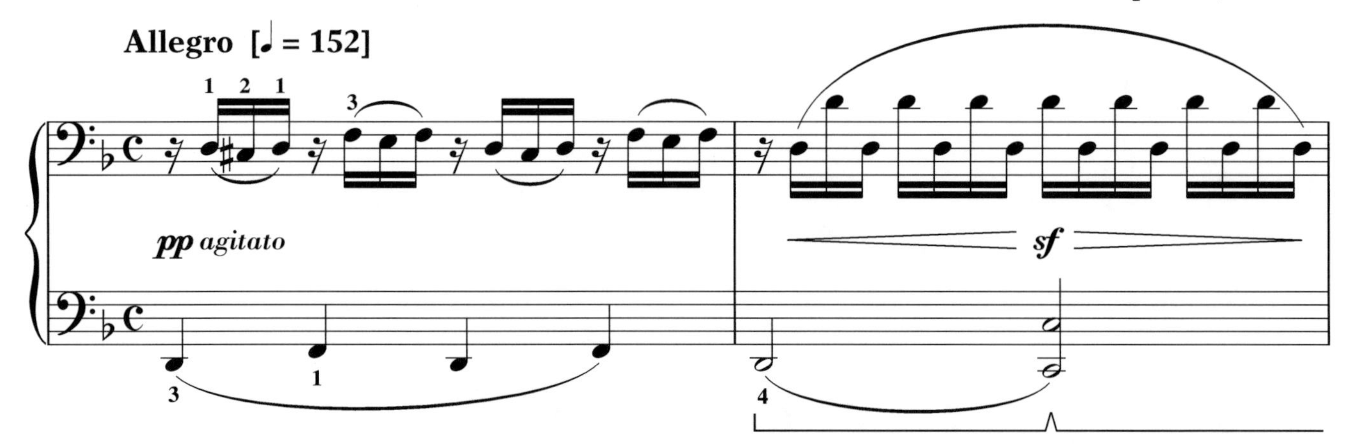

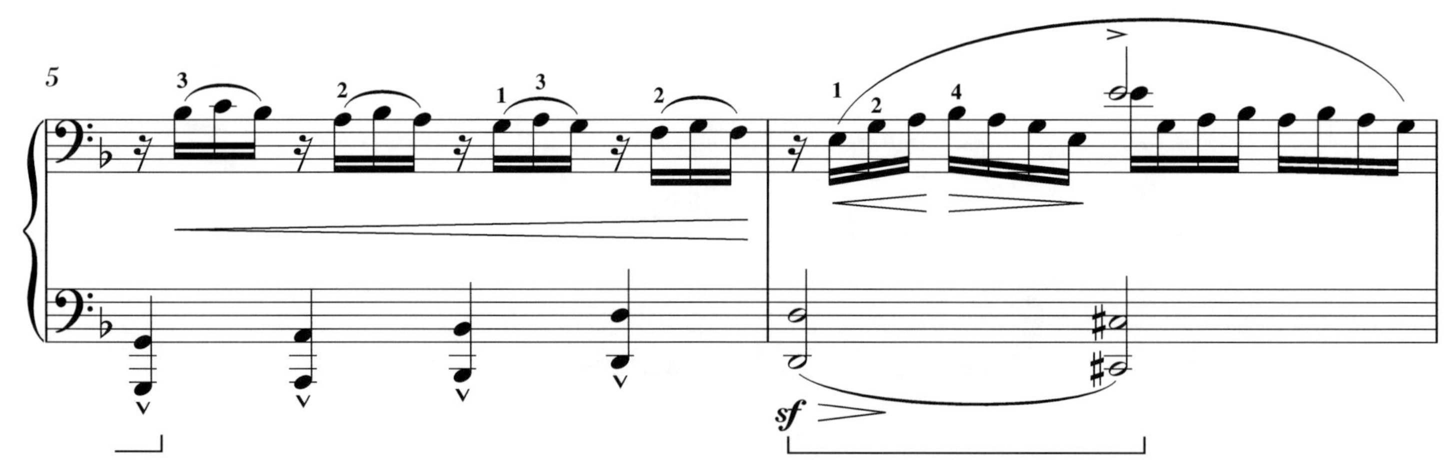

9
2.
f
3
f
1

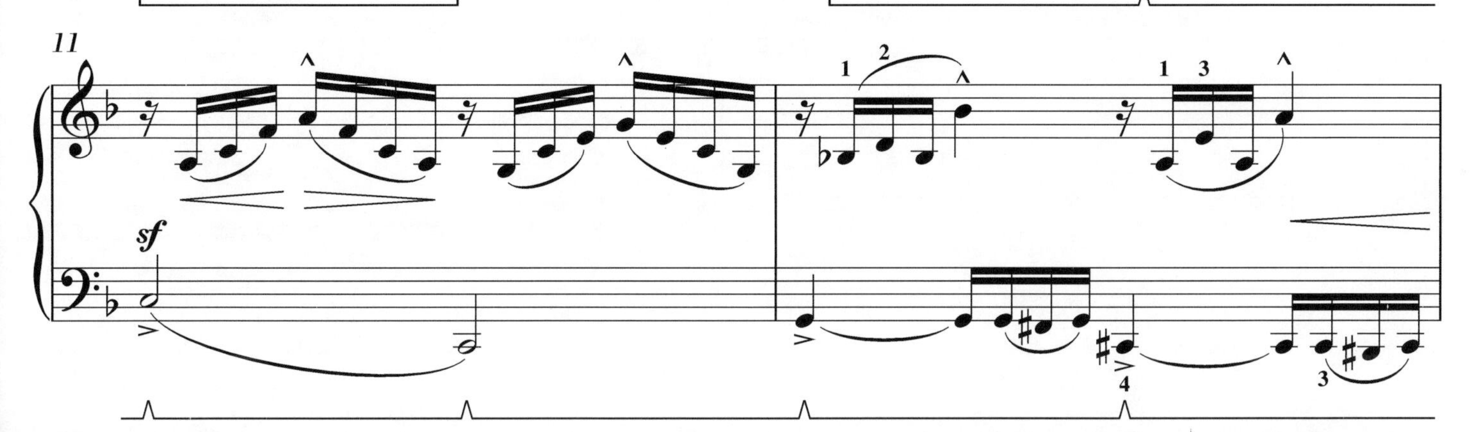
11
sf
1
2
1
3
4
3

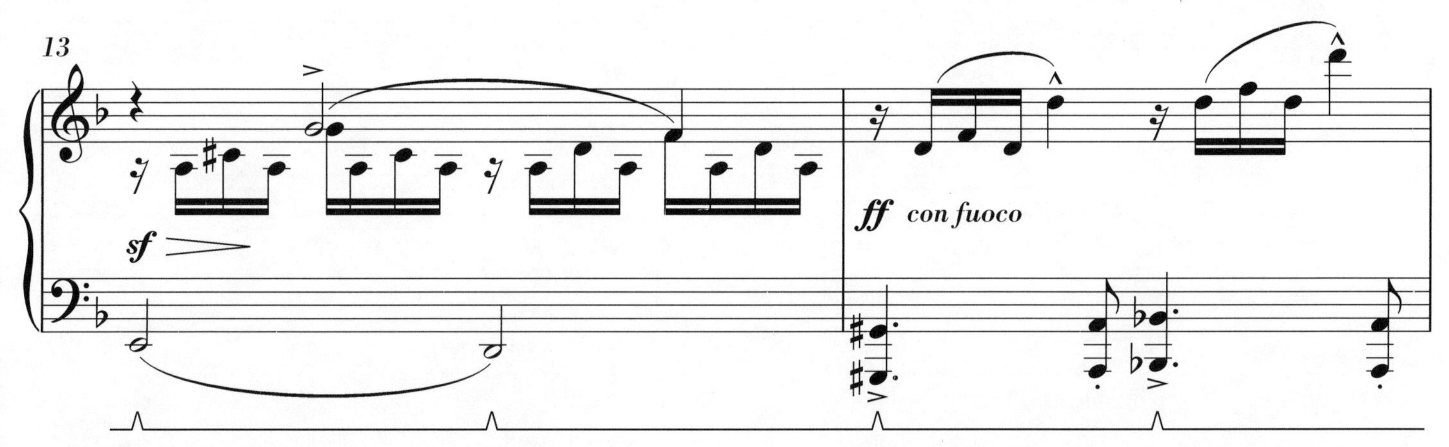
13
sf
ff con fuoco

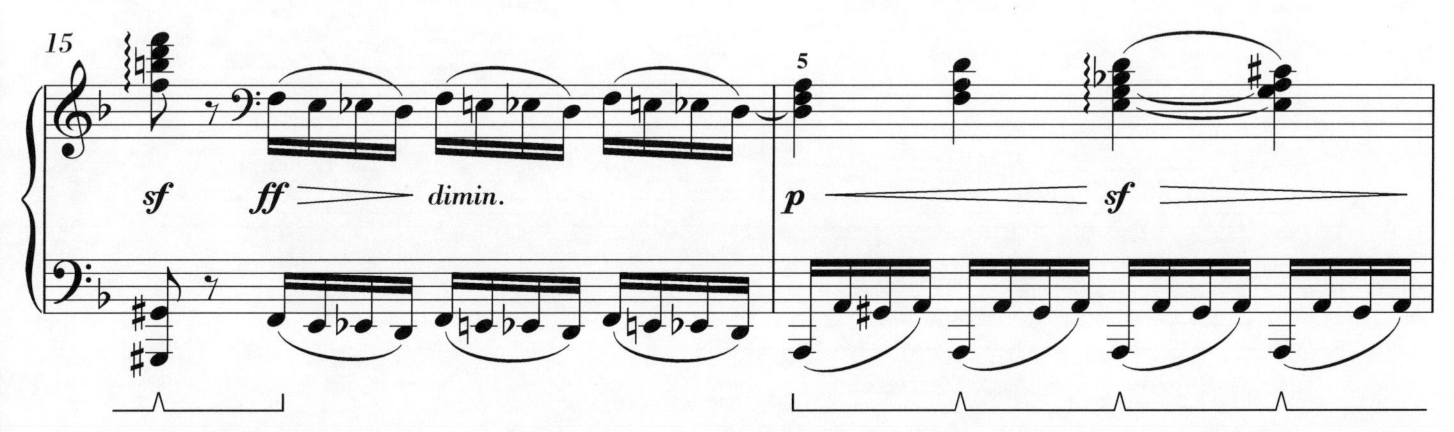
15
sf
ff
dimin.
5
p
sf

17
1.
4
5
4
cresc. e riten.
2.
p agitato

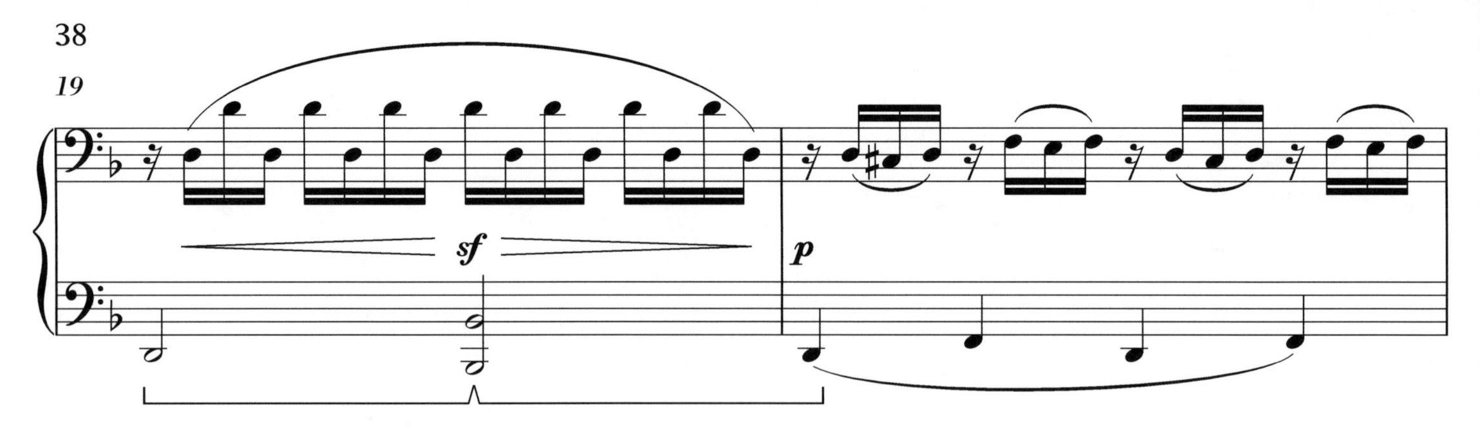
19
sf
p

21
a tempo ma un poco più lento
rit.
sf
p

23
f

25
a tempo
sf
f espressivo
p riten.

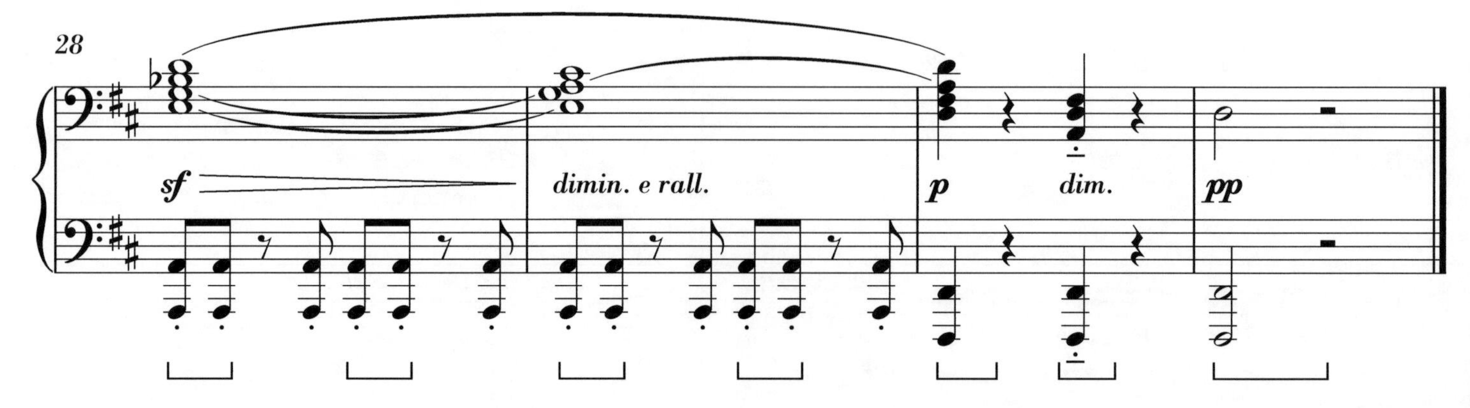
28
sf
dimin. e rall.
p
dim.
pp

LABORUM
DULCE
LENIMEN
G. SCHIRMER

Refrain du gondolier
The Gondolier's Refrain

J. Friedrich Burgmüller
Op. 109, No. 14

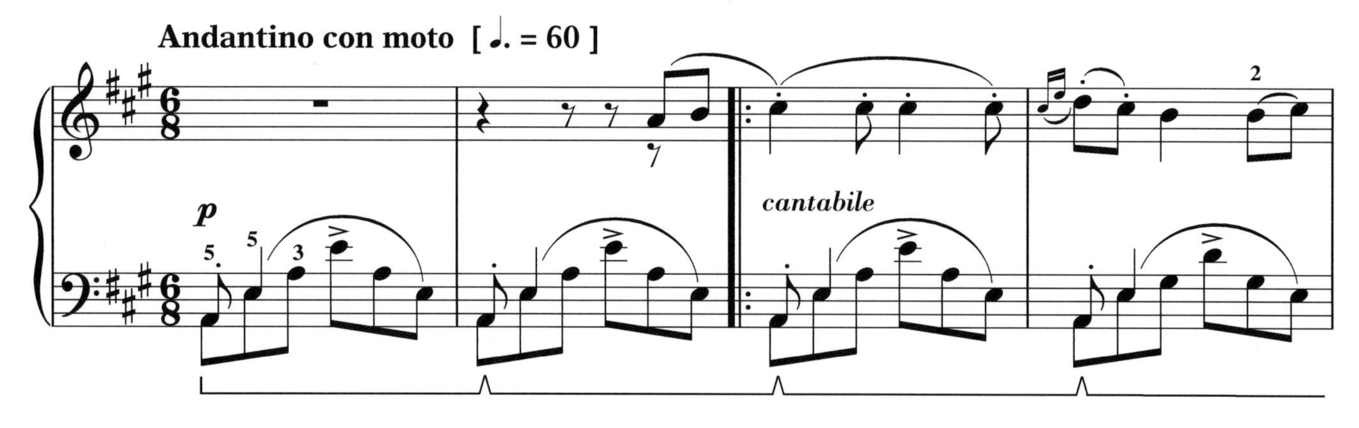

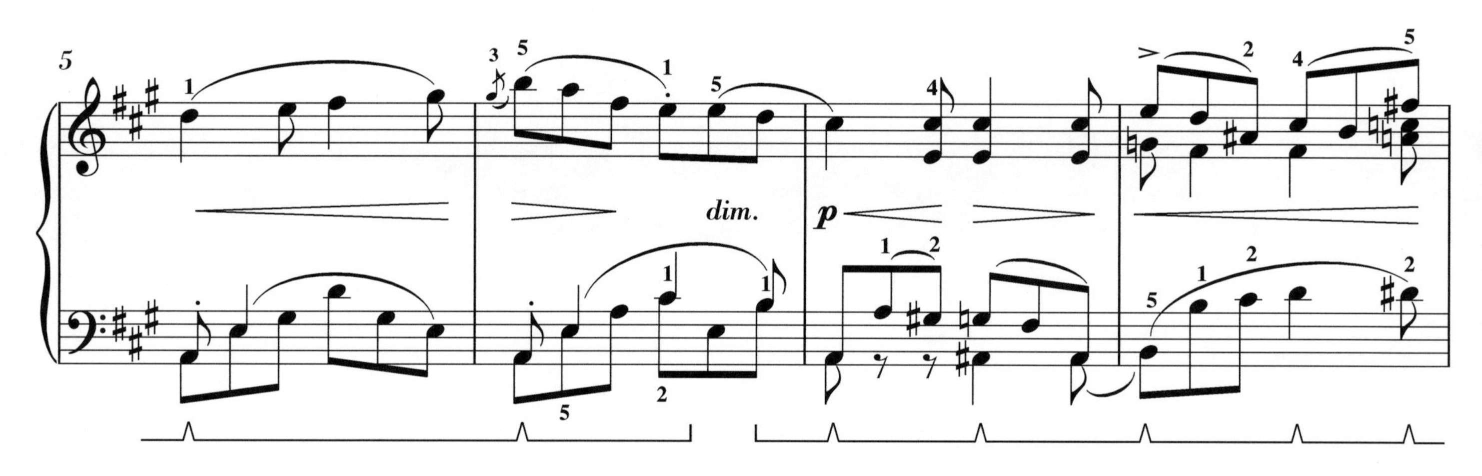

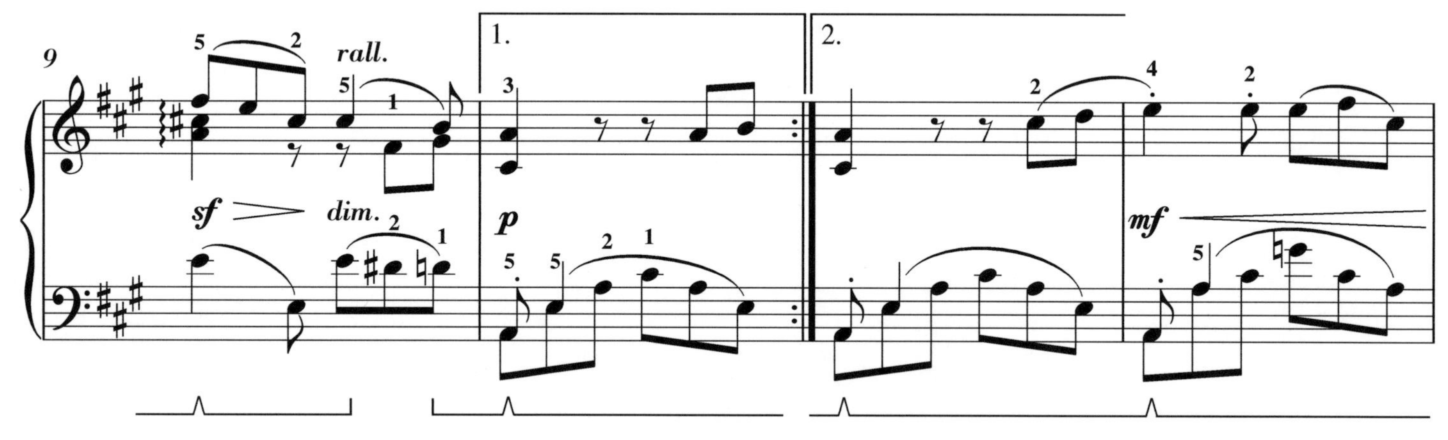

17
rall.
sf
p
dim.
a tempo
mf
p dolce

22
rall.
mf
cresc.
sf
dim.

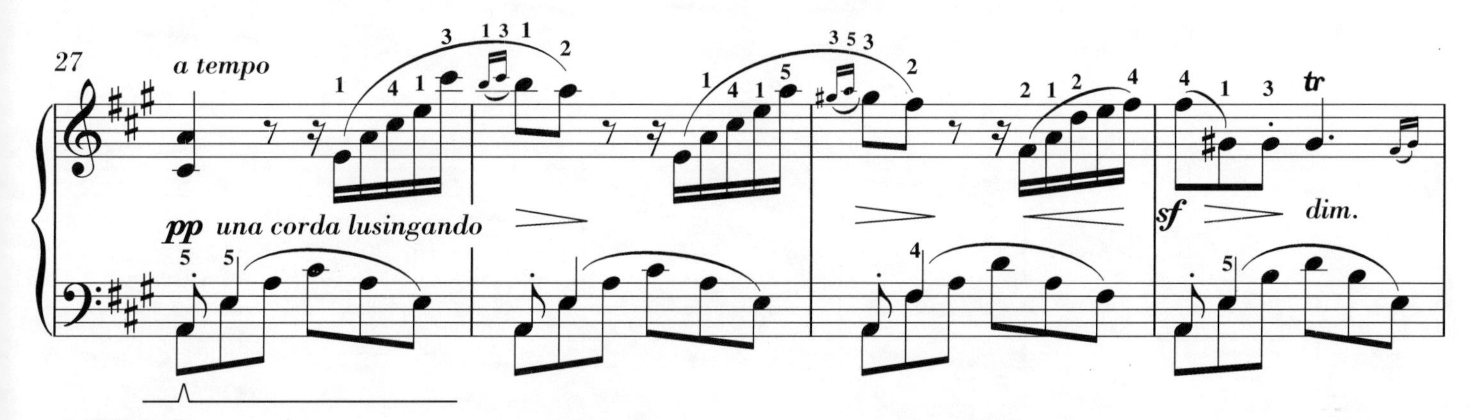
27
a tempo
pp una corda lusingando
tr
sf
dim.

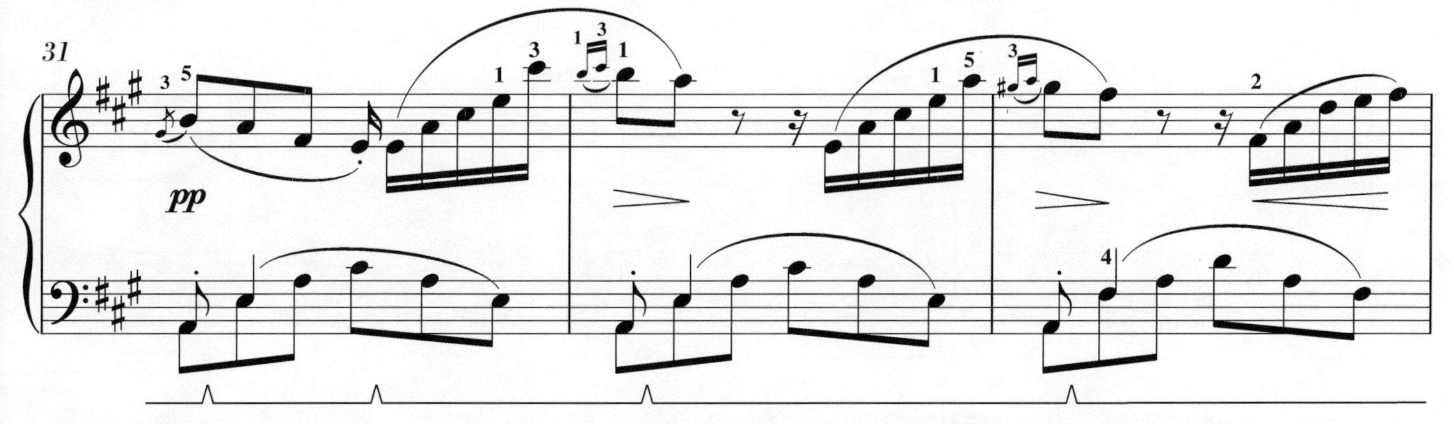
31
pp

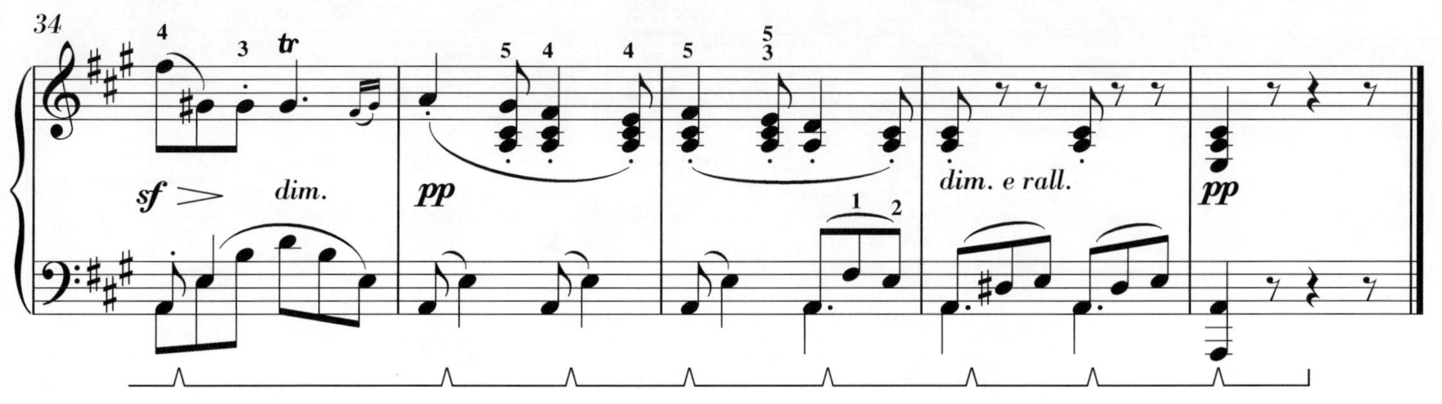
34
tr
sf
dim.
pp
dim. e rall.
pp

Les sylphes

Sylphs

J. Friedrich Burgmüller
Op. 109, No. 15

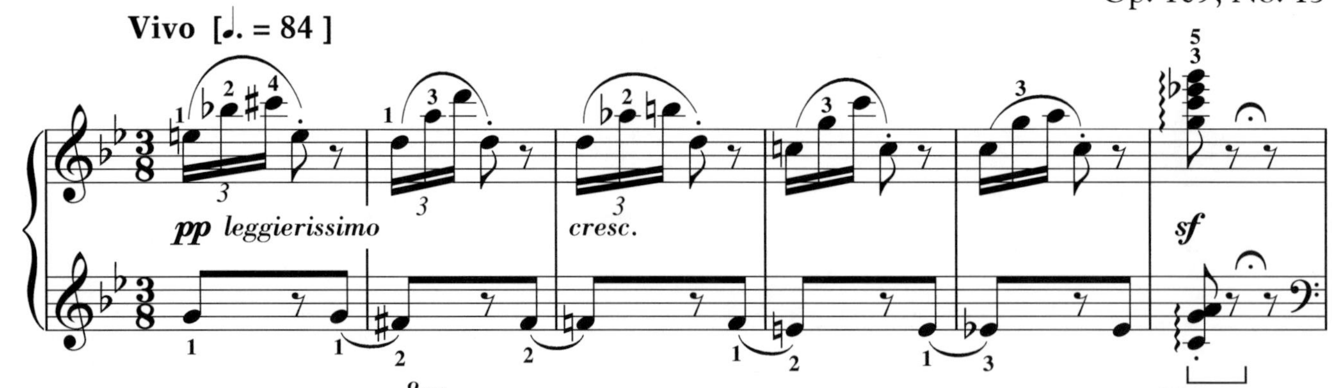

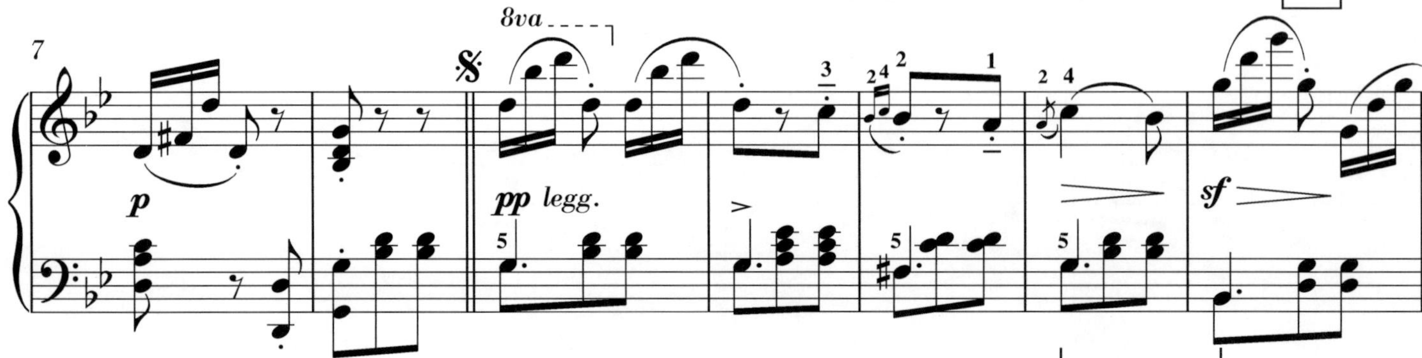

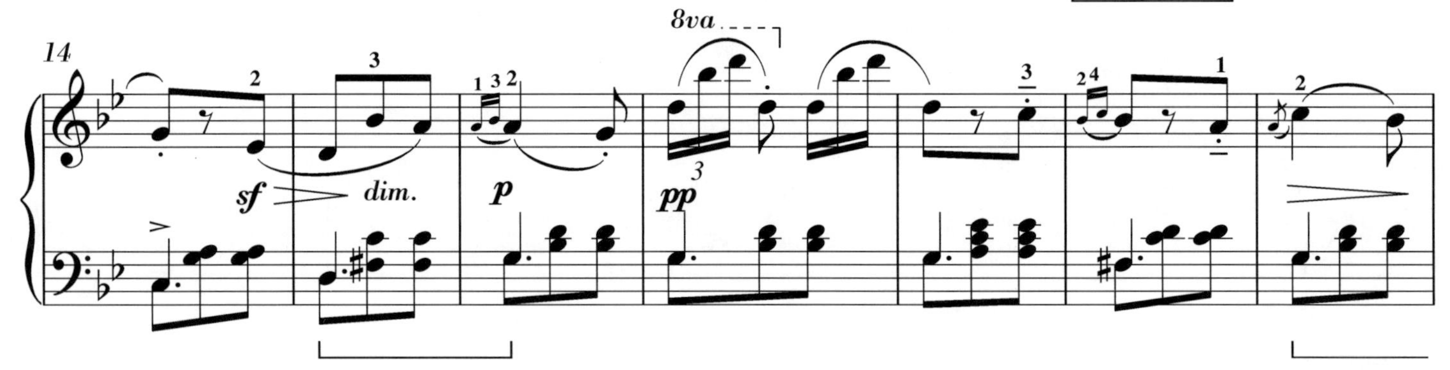

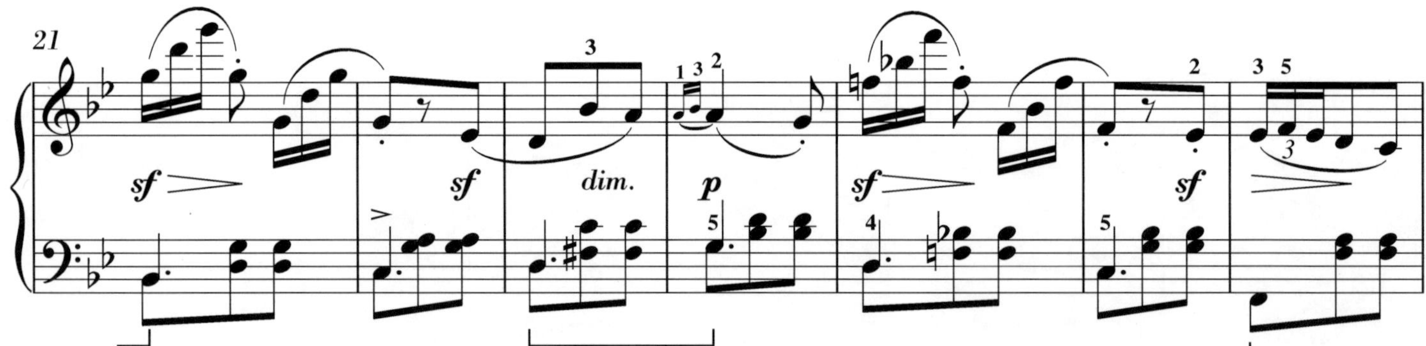

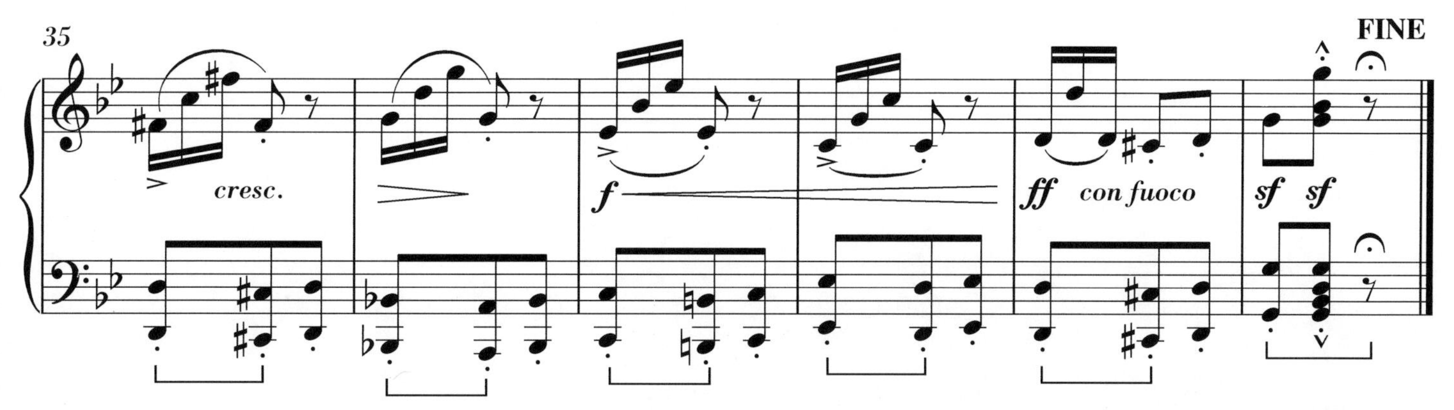
35
FINE
cresc.
f
ff con fuoco
sf sf

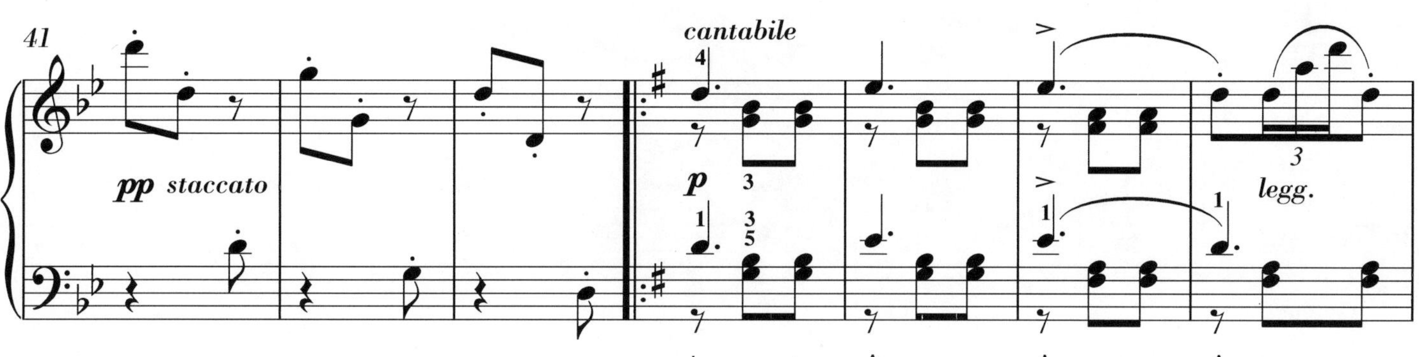
41
cantabile
pp staccato
p
legg.

48
sf
legg.
p

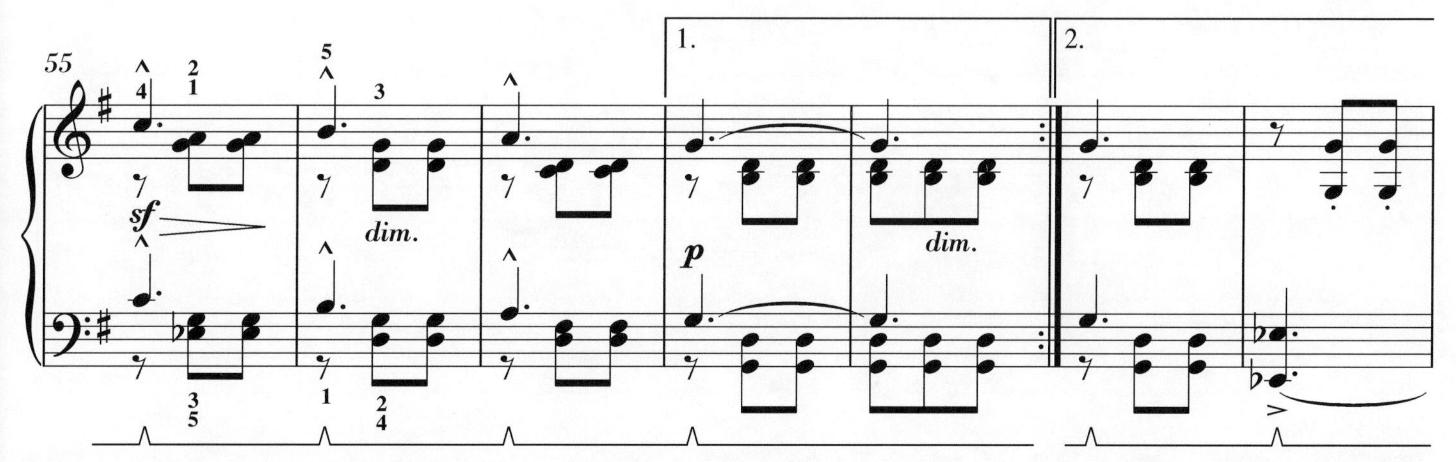
55
1.
2.
sf
dim.
p
dim.

62
D.S.
dim.
p

La séparation

Parting

J. Friedrich Burgmüller
Op. 109, No. 16

16
a tempo
p dim. rallent.
f

19
riten.
a tempo
ff
sf
dimin.
p
cresc.

22
f
f
espressivo
p

25
f

28
sf
dimin.
p
sf
sf
ff

Marche

March

J. Friedrich Burgmüller
Op. 109, No. 17

Allegro maestoso [♩ = 144]

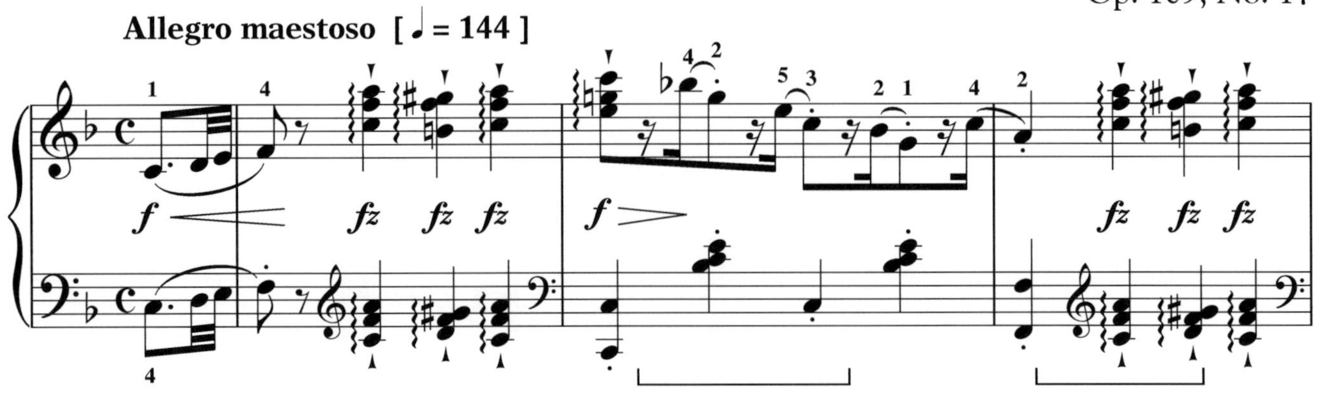

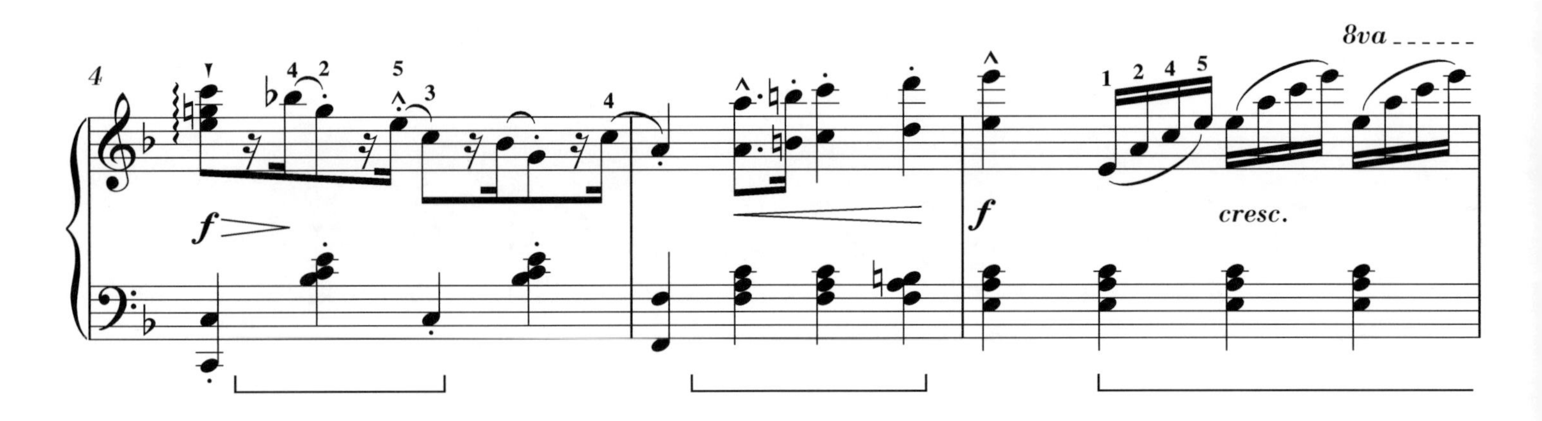

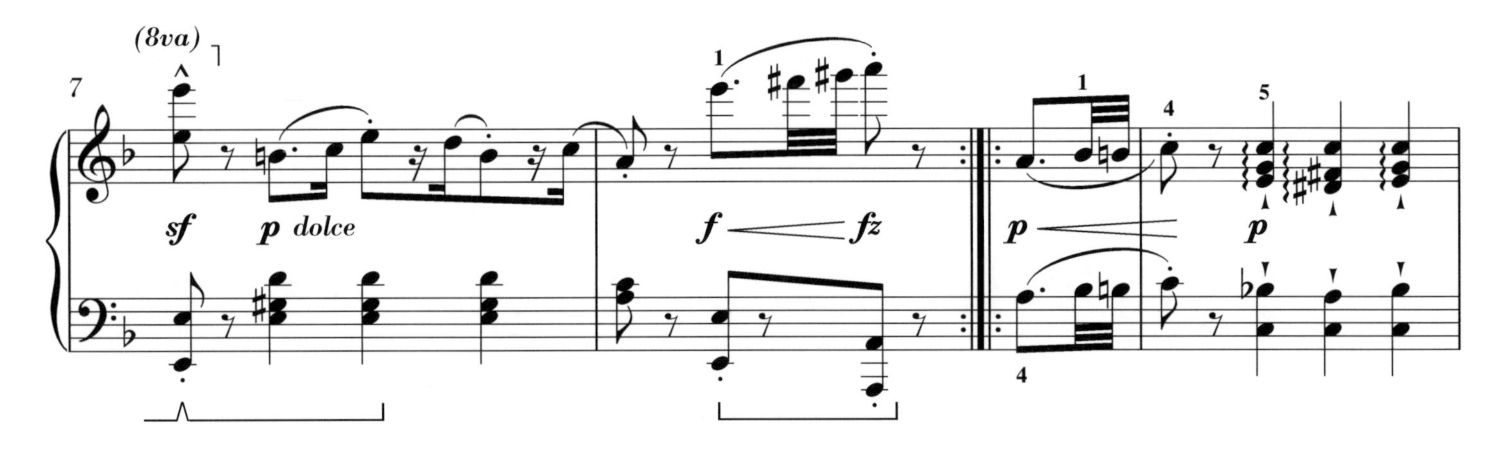

14
ff
sf

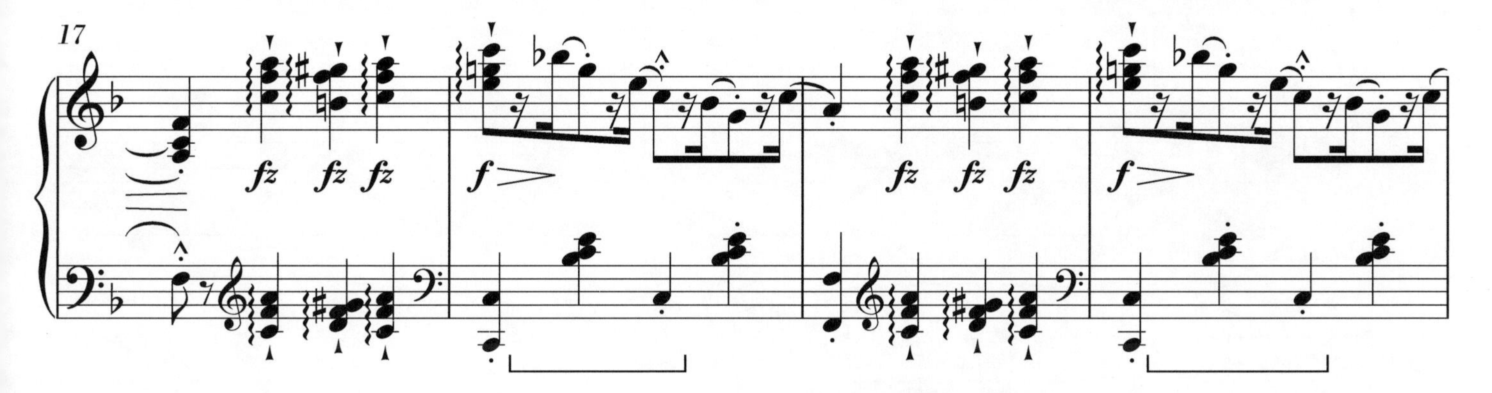
17
fz fz fz
f
fz fz fz
f

21
8va
FINE
ff
sf
l.h.
f
fz

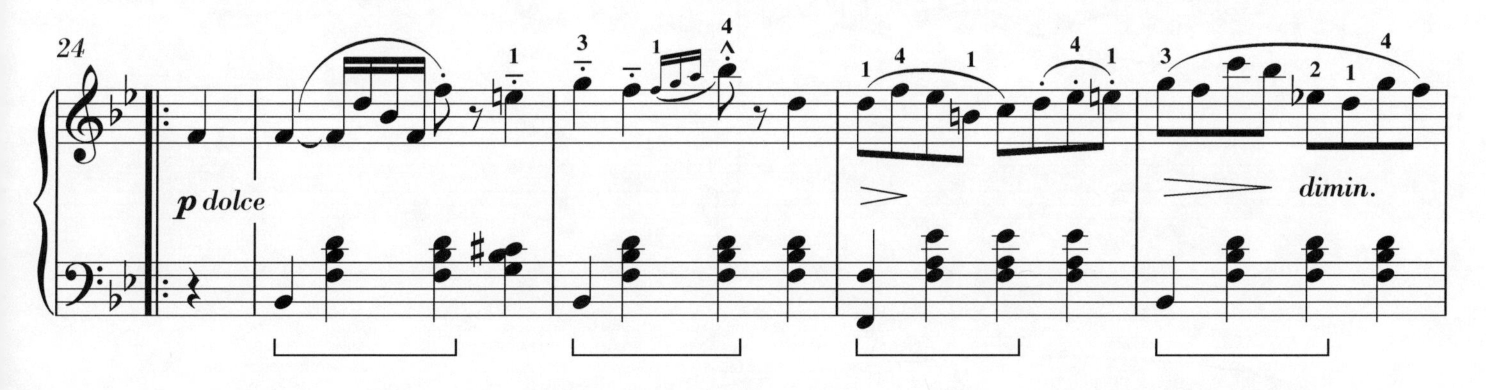
24
p dolce
dimin.

29
D.C.
p
sf
dimin.
p
poco riten.

La fileuse

At the Spinning Wheel

J. Friedrich Burgmüller
Op. 109, No. 18

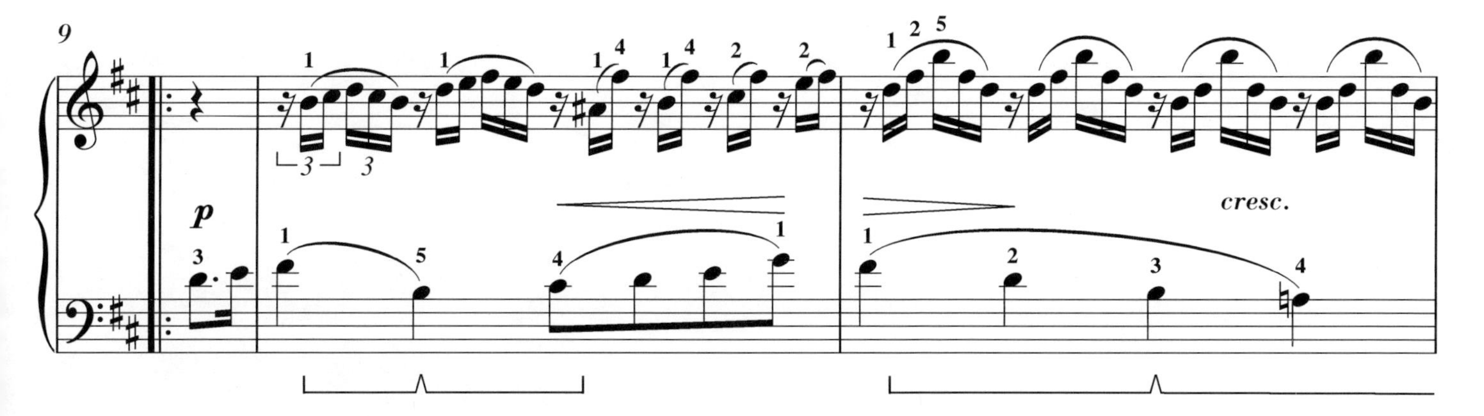
cresc.

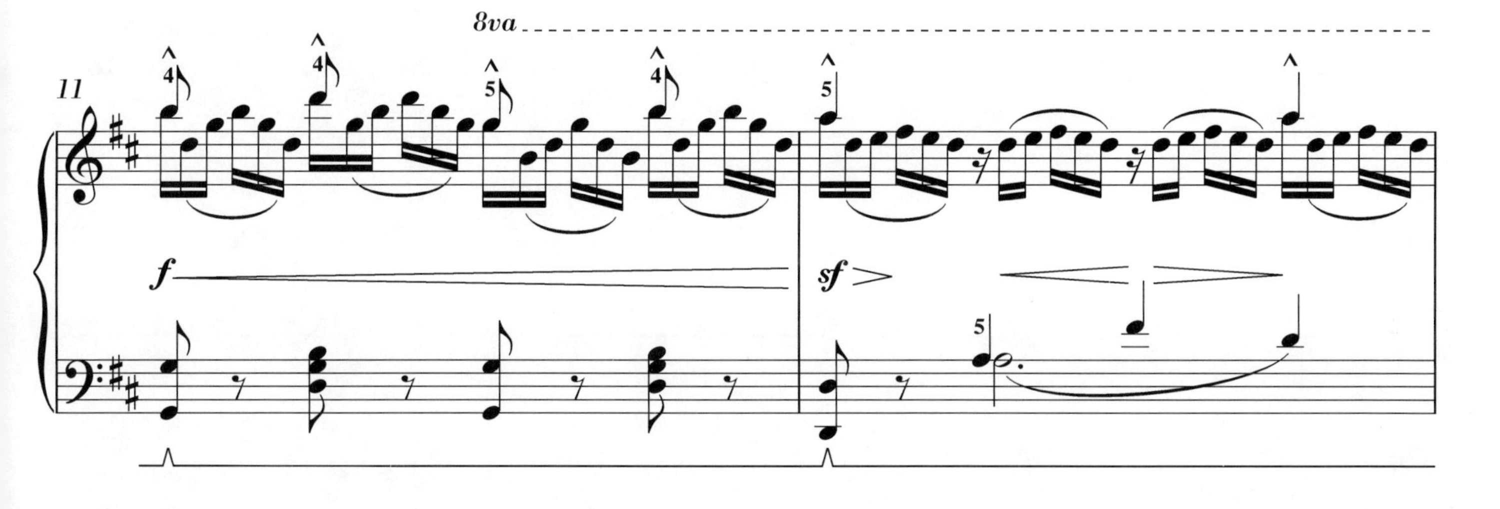
8va

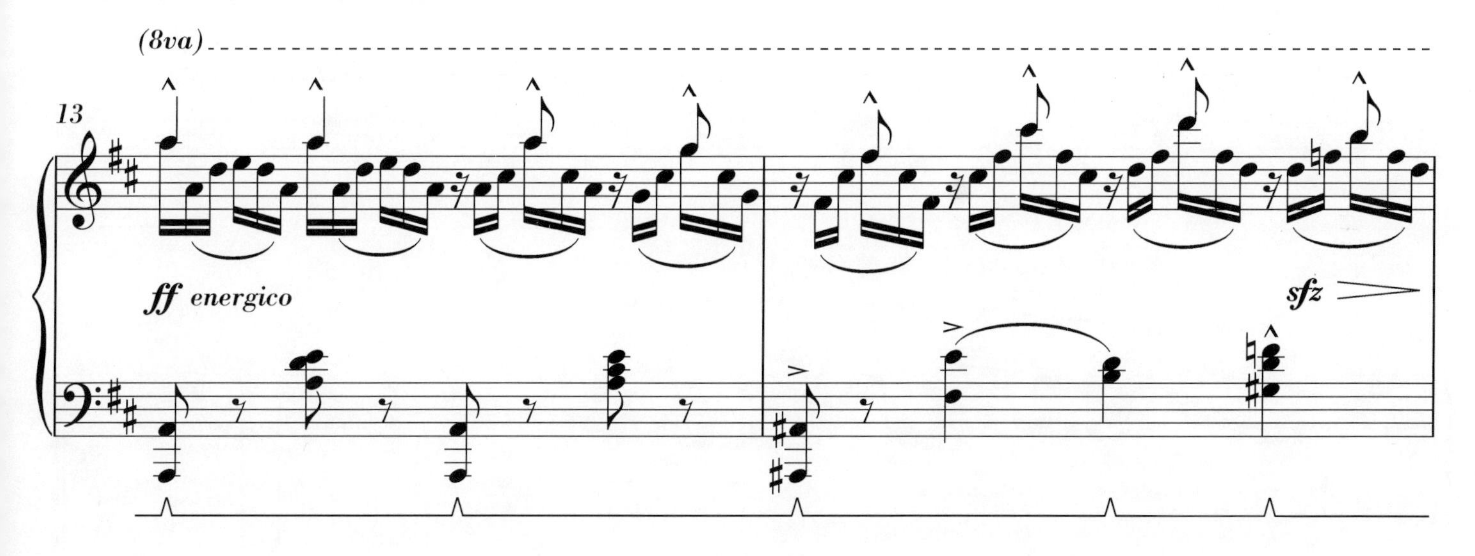
(8va)
energico

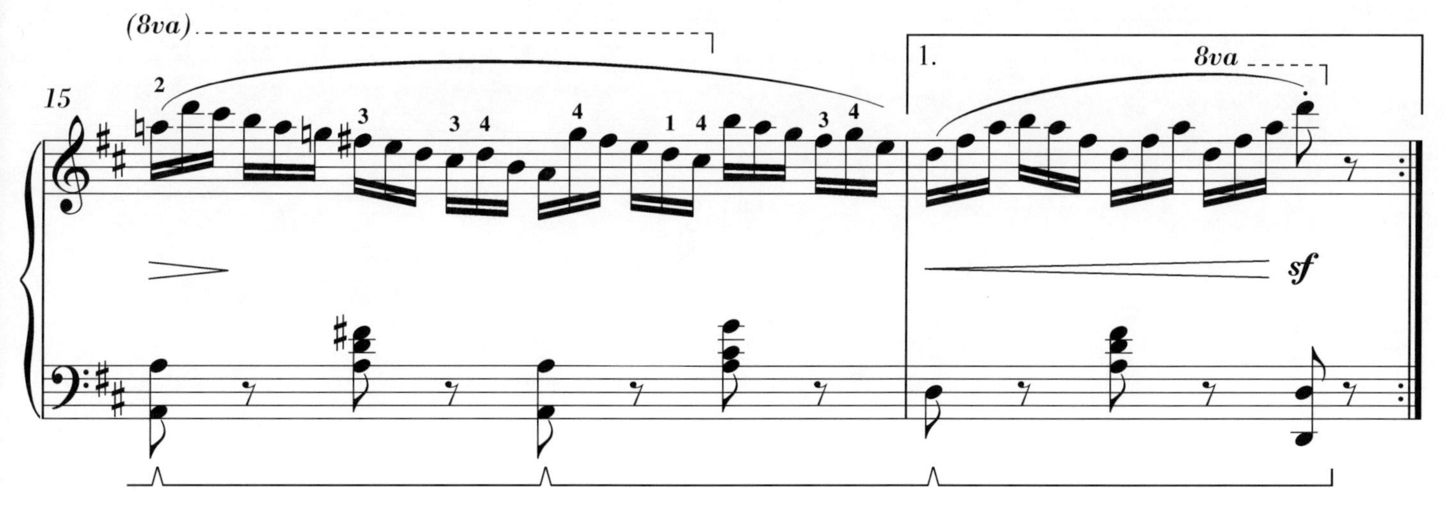
(8va)
1.
8va

17
2.
8va
pp dolcissimo

19
8va
agitato e sempre più cresc.
sf

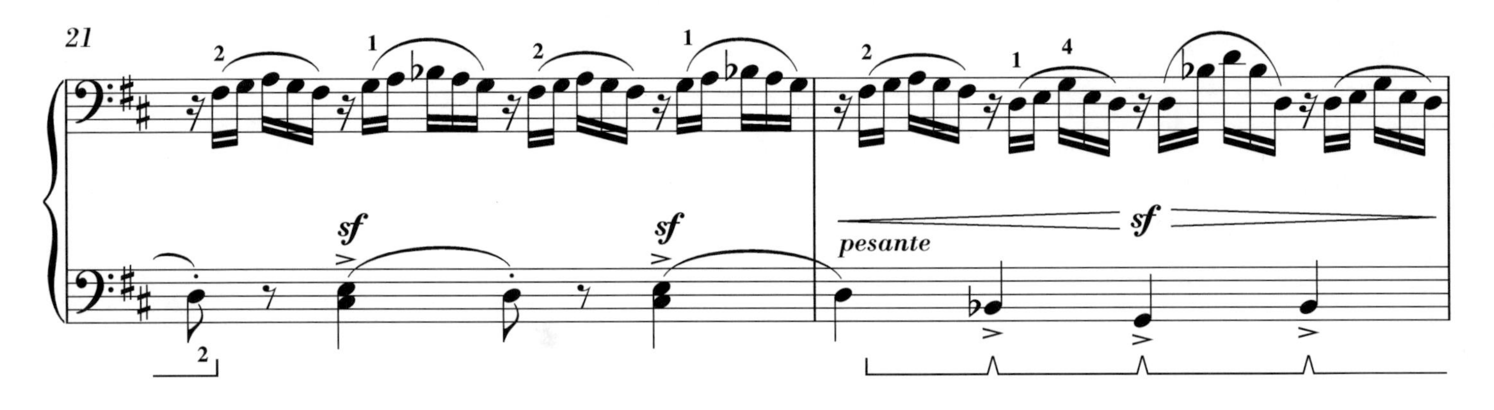
21
sf
sf
pesante
sf

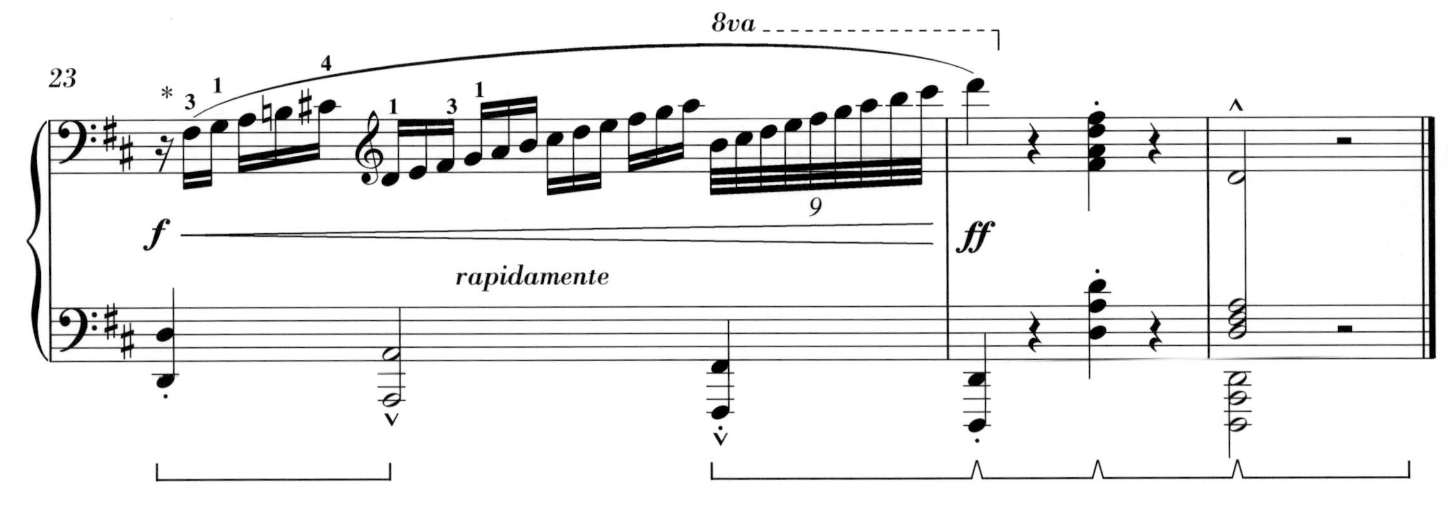
23
8va
f
9
rapidamente
ff

*
27
8va

ABOUT THE EDITOR

WILLIAM WESTNEY

Pianist **William Westney** came to prominence as the top piano prizewinner of the Geneva International Competition. He appeared thereafter in European television broadcasts and as soloist with such major orchestras as l'Orchestre de la Suisse Romande, and the Houston, San Antonio, and New Haven Symphonies. His solo recital appearances include New York's Lincoln Center, the National Gallery, Phillips Collection in Washington DC, St. John's Smith Square in London, National Public Radio ("Performance Today"), Taiwan, Korea, and a U.S. State Department tour of Italy. Critics have praised his recordings of solo and chamber works for CRI and Musical Heritage Society, and *Newsweek* magazine selected his CRI recording of Leo Ornstein's works as one of its "Ten Best American Music Recordings" of the year.

Dr. Westney holds a Bachelor of Arts degree from Queens College in New York and a Masters and Doctorate in performance from Yale University, all with highest academic and pianistic honors. He was awarded a Fulbright grant for study in Italy, and, while there, was the only American winner in auditions held by *Radiotelevisione Italiana*. His piano teachers have included Leopold Mittman, Donald Currier, Paul Baumgartner, and Claude Frank.

An internationally noted educator, William Westney has held two endowed positions at Texas Tech University—Paul Whitfield Horn Distinguished Professor and Browning Artist-in-Residence—and has been honored many times with teaching awards, including the Yale School of Music Alumni Association's prestigious "Certificate of Merit" and Texas Tech's highest honor, the Chancellor's Council Distinguished Teaching Award.

As part of its Senior Scholar program under the Council for International Exchange of Scholars (Fulbright Commission), the U.S. State Department sent Dr. Westney to seven universities in Korea in 2006. For the 2009-10 academic year, the University of Southern Denmark named him to an interdisciplinary residency as Hans Christian Anderson Guest Professor.

Dr. Westney's unique "Un-Master Class" performance workshops were described as "fascinating" in a featured *New York Times* article. They are in demand throughout the United States and abroad, and are frequently held at such prominent centers as the Aspen School (Aspen), Peabody Conservatory (Baltimore), Kennedy Center (Washington D.C.), Royal Conservatory (Toronto), Cleveland Institute (Cleveland), Tanglewood Institute (Boston), Royal College of Music (London), *Universität für Musik und darstellende Kunst* (Vienna), and the Juilliard School (New York).

Amadeus Press released William Westney's first book, *The Perfect Wrong Note*, in fall 2003 to critical acclaim. According to the *Library Journal*, it is a "well-thought-out approach to music instruction to which many aspire, but which few attain," and *American Record Guide* described it as "refreshing and rewarding."